MY ANGELS, MY GIRLS

By
Kellianne M. Peterson

My Angels, My Girls

PRINTED IN THE UNITED STATES OF AMERICA & DISTRIBUTED WORLD-WIDE

Second Edition: ©2009
First Edition: ©2008
ISBN: 978-0-9822657-9-6

Introduction

How many people have you met in life that speak of their pets as children and are chastised for it? Oh, they say, "it's only a cat, a dog, a horse, or even a rabbit." Or some other tiny creature... But what do these people know? They know nothing; in fact, they are missing out on one of the greatest gifts of all, the unconditional love of an animal. Some appreciate the loyalty of a pet, and to others they are a member of their family. Me, I cannot call them a mere pet or a member of my family for they are far more. They are my angels and without them life would not be as heartfelt and colorful as it has been, continues to be and sadness would not be as bearable. Most of all, if not for the love and loyalty of my one special angel I would not even be here to tell their stories.

My Angels, My Girls

For these reasons, every time someone says to me they are just dogs. I snicker or I shed a tear. I pity the person who does not know, is unable to open their heart wide enough or because of circumstances beyond their control is unable to know the innocence and untainted love of a pet or animal and I have a small giggle to myself of how blessed I have been, to have the unconditional perplexing love of our little four-legged human beings as I like to call them, not once but three times.

Laugh, as you will, I don't care, *my angels, my girls,* are all that I need to get me through this world. Open your heart, to an animal one day and see, the world is a much better place with the hilarious, stupendous love a furry four-legged friend can bring. The next time someone says to you "it's only a cat, a dog, a horse or even a rabbit, or some other tiny creature" you can have a snicker, a giggle or shed a tear for that person that doesn't realize the blessing of the gifts you have received from the love of a pet who became a part of your life and brought you through your years.

Each of my girls has brought to my life such a light and unequivocal happiness that I could write for days about each of them. Each is an Angel in her own right and each came to me through different circumstances. They all have their quirks, personalities, likes and dispositions but I love all of them more than anything and my world would not be complete without them. Laugh if you will, but I have numerous, amusing and amazing stories of why I could never call my girls, dogs. To be completely honest, my friends, take a look around, sometimes our four-legged friends are more human than we are.

My Angels, My Girls

Let's be honest, people. When would an animal stab you in the back, hold a grudge, or kill for no reason? Animals, especially those that are domesticated, want to be loved, to please, and they don't hold grudges; their love is basically unconditional. Yet sadly, some people brutalize these innocent creatures. Hopefully, someday everyone will see how unique and beautiful all animals are both domesticated and wild. They will see how loving they are and what a blessing they are. If you are lucky enough to have a pet, do not think of it as ownership but as a companionship and treat them as a member of your family.

For those of you who already are blessed with the love of a pet and understand how special that feeling is, never feel embarrassed by what people say because there are plenty of us out here. We probably outnumber those who have not been touched by the love of a pet (or are too stubborn or cool to admit it) and continue to spread the word no matter how goofy they think we are. "Animals have feelings too, and our pets are little people with their own personalities."

As for me, they are everything to me. They are My Angels, My Girls and these are their stories.

My Angels, My Girls

Table of Contents

MY ANGELS,
MY GIRLS

This book is dedicated to my family, friends,

all the people who helped make this book

happen and of course GOD without all things

could not be possible and my little Angels.

I would also like to make a special dedication

to the unsung heroes out there who every day,

go out, save, heal, foster, volunteer and do

whatever it takes to protect our animals both

domesticated and wild.

1

REM REM

April 5, 2002. I was in my bathroom. It was morning. The day before I had been released from the hospital for a complicated migraine ...at least that is what they thought it was. My elderly father was downstairs making breakfast. The next thing I remember is my REM REM licking my face, trying to lift me up, and dragging me out of the bathroom. The whole time howling. Her howl was the sound of a wolf in pain. A defender wolf crying to summon help, but not leaving my side; until assistance arrived. I could not move. I had suffered a stroke. I would have died that day if she had not saved me. She never once thought of leaving me.

The days following my first stroke Remi proved her loyalty and love to me more than any other human being. She could feel my pain. There are medical studies that show that animals can feel people's pain and anticipate seizures; and I am here to tell you she felt everything that I went through. I had seizures while I slept when I first came home, I would wake up with her lying across me trying to keep me safe. Her main goal was making sure I was okay. She was the perfect therapy dog and she was my life, of course with the help of my other two angels. But this is Remi's story.

The day we brought Remi home, my husband called her *his* dog. He said, "You have your dog. She is mine and I'm training her. She isn't going to be spoiled, like Georgia". Georgia is my other little angel and Sydney too, their stories are for another time. I didn't care at that point. I had my dog and I was afraid that I was going to be allergic to Remi. You see, Remi had a different smell and coat. I believe now that maybe she could have been part wolf although her pedigree was Siberian Husky. She didn't smell like Georgia, who is an American Eskimo. She did not have the same smell as Sydney, a Siberian husky who came to live with us later. She had this different smell and she was so enormous, so I thought "let my husband have his dog." I had Georgia. Little did I know what she would come to mean to me, what she would teach me about love, how I would fight my husband for her in the divorce, and how she would become my life.

Remi was soon nicknamed REM REM, among many other names. She was the most beautiful Siberian Husky you would ever see! She was built like a wolf with a shiny, thick dark grey and white coat. When she was a pup, we never thought she would grow into her paws because they were so massive! She had the most stunning blue eyes. Almost violet; my neighbor described them as Liz Taylor's eyes. She said, "You should have named her "Lizzy." But "Remi" definitely fit her.

My ex-husband always wanted to train her. And he loved her, yes he did. But she, like me, wanted to be shown love and care. REM REM did not want to be trained; she did everything at her own pace. Crate training was a disaster. We would put her in the crate at bedtime and she would howl so we let her out. We would put her in the crate during the day while we were at work so that she wouldn't mess in the house. She would have the whole crate torn apart by the time I would get home and you could hear her wailing outside. We had done the same things that we did to train Georgia that worked with Georgia, but nothing worked. REM REM followed her own drummer. Training, including housebreaking, was something that would prove to be something she would decide would be done on her time. Yes, she finally housebroke herself, but by that time I had learned you should not have rugs in your home if you share your abode with Huskies. Remi was always sneaky about it too, you always had to wear a pair of shoes around the house when she was a pup or you might come up with wet socks as one of my friends found out one morning; but she would just give you this look and you couldn't help but laugh at her.

Remi always had her little problems but she never would let anyone know and she always got herself into trouble. When she was about three months old she ate a sock and almost died. She kept hiding in the house I kept looking for her and pulling her out of the most inconspicuous places. Places that a dog would go because they think they are going to die, and they want to just go there, cry themselves to sleep and just let it all be over. Oh no, I was not going to let that happen. I would drag her out from underneath the water heater and the vents in the basement. Any place she would hide I would find her. I carried her to the vet, the dead weight that she was. My husband had given up hope. He said "puppies like this are sometimes just born with things wrong with them - just

6

let her go". I prayed and I knew it wasn't anything congenital; it wasn't her intestines all wrapped up like they told us. I was right. It was a sock she had eaten, and a case of hookworm so I nursed her back to health. And from that moment on my husband might have called her his dog, but she and I had a special bond a bond that would never be broken even by death.

My sweet REM REM... The sock was just the first of her ridiculous behaviors that would always end with her at the vet or in some sort of trouble.

REM REM always liked to play and run; one of her favorite things to do was to chase bees and see if she could catch them. They were always too quick for her; but one day she thought she was slick, hiding in the bushes, she darted out like a bullet, catching an unsuspecting bee who was pollinating a nearby rose bush. Poor Remi, she was so happy she had finally captured her prey until I heard a yelp. Her prey had turned the tables on her. It was back to the vet again as poor little REM REM's snout grew twice the size of her face due to the stinger right in the tip of her nose. Through the years, she continued to chase her bees, but I think she gained a respect for them that day.

Siberian Huskies - you gotta love them! They do not like to be confined at all. Our first house had a three-foot high chain link fence. As soon as Remi started to grow, she realized that it was a mere hop for her to scale it, so up went the chicken wire - about three feet of it all around. Our thinking was, "She won't try to get out now," yeah right! I was looking out the kitchen window, and there goes Remi climbing with each of her little toes in each of the chain links up the fence - and over - and down the back street. The problem was that I was now caged in and I couldn't hop that fence. I had to run around the front, get in the car, and chase her down before she gets hurt. The best thing about Remi at that time was she never went far, and as soon as she heard you call her name, she knew she was in trouble. She wouldn't come back, but she would sit and cower down wherever she was and wait. The worst thing, however, was that she would be scared. And become dead weight; afraid that her father would punish her and yell at her too much. So you had to practically drag her into the car, like a screaming little child, howling all the way home.

She used to think she was funny; the world's biggest spoiled lap dog. If it happened to be a beautiful night, she wouldn't want to come in. She would play dead. Or she would fall asleep outside, and God Forbid you tried to get her up to come in. She would roll on her back or her side, or curl up. You were not getting her to go anywhere unless you carried her. In the end she would win and she would be carried like a big oversized lap dog. Eventually, when she got too big she started to get dragged but she didn't care. She just didn't want to put forward the effort of walking so I would pull her (until she got her stretch), which is what I think she wanted anyway. Then she would roll over and mosey on in.

Remi loved sleeping outside. But along with two other dogs, and me still recuperating from my stroke, my father used to forget about her sometimes. He would think she was with me, and I would think all of the girls were downstairs; then I would wake up in the middle of the night hearing her howl. She would make a lamenting cry of death because he left her in the yard. I would slowly make it downstairs and let her in and she would give me a little glare like, "Mommy how could you?" I would hold her and give her a treat because I felt so bad, but then she would kiss me and we would both go up to bed, and back to sleep (after she got done howling at her sisters for not telling me that she was outside) At least I think that was why she was howling at them.

As I said earlier in this story she had her idiosyncrasies. The biggest, comical, and one of the most endearing of which we found out at one of our barbecues. All day long, our guests were enjoying themselves drinking their beer or their wine and Remi would come up to them to beg (all dogs beg of course) and husky's; God love them they can be the worst, but Remi - she was begging for people's drinks. My guests they found this adorable and hilarious. I on the other hand was not so pleased. After all, it was alcohol.

Later on that night, as I was cleaning up and throwing the dirty paper plates and half filled cups of beer in the trash, I noticed that all the cups that had wine in them were missing. And so was my REM REM. First, I ran in the house. Georgia was inside but no Remi. Then, I almost had a heart attack. Had someone let her out of the yard? Is my baby lost?

Terrible thoughts went through my mind. Then, from the far corner of the yard by the horseshoe pits I heard, "Buuuurrrrrrrrrrrrrrrrrrp!" The biggest belch I ever heard come out of a dog or a human being. There she was, curled up in the horseshoe pits with every half empty wine glass that she could find. My REM REM was a wino! The next day as she lay there on the couch motionless I was consumed with worry. I ran to her side and she looked up at me with bloodshot eyes, let out another enormous burp, then a little growl, and she pulled the blanket and her paw over her head. As if to say "Get away from me Mommy, I have a hangover." I think she took after her father that way and had learned to mimic him too.

So, over the years I would try to keep alcohol away from her. She liked beer and wine but her favorite was hot Japanese sake. She was constantly tipping glasses over, licking the contents off the floor, or the table, or the person she decided to spill it on I finally lost the battle with her and gave her a small little glass of her own. She would then sit there happily and join in the conversation, and not bother anyone for another glass. She just wanted to be included in the fun. After all she was just a four-legged furry human. She even slept like a human being. Almost every time I would catch her sleeping on her favorite couch she would be on her back, legs sprawled wide open, arms crossed over, head tilted to the side snoring away. Not exactly the position for a little lady, but then she wasn't prissy like her older sister Georgia, who Heaven forbid would never be caught sleeping in a position like that. Sneaking up on Remi was a sight. She would roll over ever so quickly, let out a big sneeze and look at you with this indignant glare, "How dare you disturb me, you ignorant people?"

She was a Husky; big in every way, built like a wolf, and never did she bark - but she would talk your ear off. And if she did bark, you knew she meant business, but she never harmed a soul. She would just let you know. My husband learned that toward the end of our marriage. He came home drunk one night and we were having another one of our screaming matches when REM REM got right between us and let out the most ferocious bark I had ever heard. That was the first time she had ever barked and the first time my husband

realized Remi was no longer his dog. She did not lunge

at him or snarl but she stood her ground and she made

it clear that she would not allow anyone to hurt me or

speak to me in that manner again.

2

THE LEADER OF THE

PACK

She enjoyed being the leader of the pack; one of her favorite things to do being a Husky with that wolf mentality was to howl. Some nights she would have us all howling. It was a song, and she would be so proud that she started it! Our neighbors probably thought that we were nuts, but I didn't care; we were happy. Me and my Angels, my little pack all howling in unison.

I regress back to her younger years when I was having a cement patio put in my backyard. It was one of those Kodak moments. I wish to this day I had a camcorder running. Remi, and Georgia, and I were outside and I told Remi and Georgia to stay off of the wet cement. They both just cocked their heads. They both had their leashes on in case I had to quickly grab them so neither of them could venture onto the cement. Georgia kept sniffing around the new patio, Georgia being the inquisitive one. I turned around, and the next thing I knew REM REM had her by the leash and was literally walking her around the perimeter of the yard. Yes, picture it... Remi walking Georgia! It was so adorable. All the while she was making sure that Georgia stayed clear of that cement. REM REM, the leader of the pack.

Remi's howling was definitely that of a wolf; loud and powerful. She may have been the middle child, but whether she was crying, trying to protect me, reprimanding one of her siblings (which she did quite often) or summoning for help, she ruled the pack, after her mother of course. Until the day she reprimanded me for the entire world to see, and I learned my lesson.

She was quite tiny, maybe two or three months old and we were on the way back home from one of her vet check ups. Remi always hated the car; she would squirm around in the back seat, the front seat or all over. While I was driving during this particular ride, she wiggled her way under my feet and the car seat, and got stuck. She then proceeded to cry. Luckily I was able to pull over, get her out and position her in a seatbelt in the front seat next to me. She felt better then. I continued on my way and realized I had to stop to pick up tickets for a show. My little girl was napping at this point. I pulled into the parking spot, opened the window a bit and ran into the store. I knew I wasn't going to be long or I never would have left her in there alone because I do not believe in leaving an animal in a car. I was in the store a total of five minutes I came out and all I heard was this horrific screaming, howling and crying. REM REM had woken up in the car and I was not there. The people in the parking lot were looking at me like I was the most despicable human being on the planet, and at that moment I felt like the most despicable person in the universe. I ran to the car and threw open the door and just hugged and kissed away her tears. I had learned my lesson; even a minute was too much.

Yes, I truly believe REM REM and my other two angels have taught me to be a better person. They have shown me that love has no boundaries and the depth of true unconditional love and understanding. Remi actually tried to speak English. She was funny sometimes she reminded me of the cartoon character Scooby Do the way she would try to speak and understand. She loved watching TV and I think at times she actually understood it. She had her favorite programs and those she did not enjoy so much. The same was true of her musical tastes. If she liked it, she would lie in front of the stereo and listen; if not she would howl, get up, and walk away.

She would also let you know if she liked you or if she didn't. You always could tell; if she did, you got kisses and hugs. Sometimes if you weren't careful you would even get bowled over by because she was so strong. She loved people, and loved being the center of attention. Remi was also a bit jealous of her siblings.

She had to be first; she had to be next to me at all times. After all she was my protector, and she was not about to share me with anyone, yet she wouldn't harm a fly. Now, if she didn't like you, she wouldn't bark or howl, or do anything that most dogs do. She would just sit across from you and stare you down with this look as if she was sizing you up for dinner. Then she would saunter on over and look at you, let you get a little pet in, look at you again, then casually knock your drink on you. But this time it wasn't to gain access to your drink it was to make it clear that she didn't want you in her house and for you to go home. Yes, I think I should have followed her advice a few times. She was definitely a good judge of character.

She was smart as a whip, she could open doors, figure out how to get the roast out of the pan, off the counter, without dropping the pan, mind you (so you would think the roast was still there). She knew how to cool off her hot spaghetti by flipping the plate upside down on the floor and then eating it off the floor. She would even steal your food from your plate if you weren't looking. But one day she learned her lesson with hot wings. She sat there for about 15 minutes just licking her chops and drinking water trying to get the sting out of her mouth. Yes, the poor thing never stole a scrap of food again. She could hide every bad thing she did, except when she wanted you to know. When she was trying to get away with something she would get this sneaky little walk, and she would look back at you as if to say, "Ha Ha!" or "Tehehee!" She was spoiled rotten, and she knew all she had to do was look at you with those big eyes, put her head on your lap and pet you with her paw. Yes she knew how to pet you too.

God forbid that girl ever got house broken or she ever learned how to do tricks like normal dogs. Remi would just cock her head and look at you as if to say, "Stupid human, you go fetch the ball." "I have better things to do," and she was entirely too smart about hiding her accidents. Although as she got older she decided she wanted to go out, but it wasn't because of our training; it was her decision. Yes, she was stubborn, but she would bring joy and laughter to everyone she met. Stubborn, sneaky, smart, lovable, and loyal are the words that best describe REM REM.

3

REM REM'S EMOTIONAL

SUPPORT

My second stroke was worse than my first. Whether or not it was a total stroke, TIA or the residual effects from the first, it affected areas of my brain, which left my cognitive and motor functions impaired. After leaving the hospital, I was placed in a rehabilitation center for eight weeks for physical and cognitive therapy. This was the most grueling experience of my life but if not for the therapists there I don't think I would be where I am today. However, a main part of my recovery was that I knew I had to get home to my girls. My father would put the phone to their ears every night so I could talk to them when I was finally able to speak. He told me how they were acting at home; how they would mope around the house, and how they would respond to my voice on the phone - especially Remi.

The best part of this particular rehabilitation facility was that they allowed your pets to visit you. They understood the value of animal therapy. Of course, you had to be mobile enough to go to certain areas. The day my father brought Remi to visit me was probably one of the happiest days of my life. I remember sitting in my wheelchair, in the roof top garden; it was a beautiful Indian summer day. Everyone was sitting out there with his or her visitors, enjoying the beautiful day. The wait was killing me, and my father wasn't sure she would make the car ride. Then the elevator doors opened. I saw her peak her head out; she looked confused hanging on to my father. She was scared; she ran back into the elevator because she was afraid of all the people. Then she saw me sitting in my wheelchair. It had been six weeks since she had last seen me, so she sprinted and broke from my father's grip. The other patients and visitors didn't know what to do, but she came right for me with this unbelievable smile on her face. She leapt right into my wheelchair with me, almost knocking us both over, but she didn't, and she kissed my whole face. I just hugged and kissed her too. As big as she was, she always thought she was a lap dog. From that point on, my recovery was swift. All I wanted to do was get home to REM REM and my other sweet girls.

My Angels, My Girls

My father was in a horrible accident two years ago. Once again REM REM took up the slack, checking on him, keeping her sisters in line, showing respect to her now aging older sister Georgia, and was always there to kiss away my tears and give me the support I needed. She would be there to greet me at the door, knocking me over with a big bear hug and kiss. When she would stand on her hind legs she was taller than me.

She was intimidating, beautiful, and big, but she could be shy and easily scared. Her fear of cars and her fear of strangers discounted her from being a great watchdog, but her wolf like appearance would probably frighten off any burglar, or anyone who threatened me, my father or her sisters. However, if someone knew her, things would be quite different and one of my favorite stories is her encounter with a beagle; each one protecting their turf.

My father was in an extended care facility after one of his surgeries, and all he wanted was to see REM REM, they allowed pet visits. But this hospital did have two resident therapy beagles. The beagles roamed the halls freely visiting the patients. They were precious, protective, and quite comical. If they didn't like you, or know you, they would follow you up the hall, howling and barking.

The day I brought Remi to see my father, they caught her scent right away. Of course, they were a third of her size, and they started following us to my father's room barking and howling the whole way. My big baby REM REM started crying and making a sound like a monkey, a sound she makes only when she's really scared (Monk Monk was another one of her nicknames she was dubbed as a pup). Although she was shaking and cowering behind me, we finally made it to my father's room. She immediately jumped in the bed and hid her face. The nurses had to shut the door to my father's hospital room long enough to calm down the beagles and the Monkey in order to get her out of my father's hospital bed. After all it was their house. The whole time she visited with my father she was making her monkey voice and shaking like a leaf. By the time the poor thing was finally calmed down it was time to leave. Leaving followed the same way, with Monk Monk at it again. All the nurses had to hold on to the big, bad, Beagles, and everyone was afraid of the big intimidating wolf dog who came into the hospital. But they later fell in love with her when they learned the big baby hid her head in her grandfather's hospital bed because of the big, bad, Beagles.

My father was eventually released from this facility, but the infection from his surgeries returned. Remi continued taking care of everyone, watching after dad while I was at work, and being my rock when I got home. But some things just happen, and as much as you pray, bargain, or pretend it was all a bad dream, you can't change the outcome.

My Angels, My Girls

4

THE WORST NIGHT OF

MY LIFE

Money was tight, and my father's condition was getting worse. We had decided to move to a smaller house with a bedroom on the first floor for him; he was practically confined to bed by this point. And then it happened. The worst night of my life…

As I had said previously, my father had suffered a dreadful accident which had left him all but bed ridden. It was early May 2005; I was working, and we were packing because that June we were moving into a smaller house because of my divorce and my father's condition. REM REM had just turned seven that January. I came home from work late that May evening and my father said to me "Remi needs water she has been panting all day" I looked, gave her some water and we went outside to play. She drank and appeared to be fine. We played and ran around in the yard, and then Remi just stopped. She looked at me with this glazed look in her eyes. I called her over to me; she slowly walked over, a slow stagger and kissed me. I said, "Are you okay, baby? What's the matter, girl?" She kissed me again. I hugged her a few minutes then we went inside. She drank some water and seemed okay. I said, "I know what you want you want – meatloaf!" That was one of Remi's favorite things to eat especially if she didn't feel well; that would always perk her up. She wagged her tail and went upstairs. I heated up the meatloaf thinking she was checking on my father; that had been her normal routine, as of late. Then I brought the meatloaf upstairs.

She wouldn't eat a bite. I looked at her, and I knew at that point something was terribly wrong. This was not your normal panting; her chest was heaving in and out quickly, and she couldn't catch a breath. She wouldn't eat. This all happened within an hour. I called the vet. They were closed. I got the number for the Emergency Animal Hospital in the area. I called them. They gave me directions. I was in a panic. I put her leash on her and she could barely make it down the stairs. She was so wobbly, so weak, her eyes so glazed. I kept thinking, "Why didn't I call sooner? Why didn't I realize something was so terribly wrong? Why? Why? Why? What's wrong with my baby?" I got her in the car and as we are driving she started to gag. Oh my God!

She's choking! She seems better; maybe she just got stung by a bee again. Maybe it's just an allergic reaction to something. She's fine! She has to be.

We went inside the Animal Hospital. I explained her symptoms, and that I thought something might be caught in her throat, and that she couldn't breathe and that she was gagging. They took her from me right away to check for obstructions and to x-ray.

That was the last time I saw my sweet REM REM awake.

They told me she had Pulmonary Bulla, a congenital lung defect that Siberian Huskies are at risk for. The analogy the vet gave me was that the lung explodes from the inside, like a when a tire develops a bubble in it, and has a blow out. My sweet baby was on the table for six hours as they tried to eradicate the fluid from her lungs. I tried frantically to reach her father as I sat in the holding room crying.

The Doctor finally came out and explained to me that if she had been hit by a car, maybe she would have had a chance. Or, if I could have gotten her to another Animal Hospital that had a ventilator where they could completely open her up, she would have a better chance. But she would most likely not survive the drive, and there was only a 20 percent chance of survival with the surgery. And she would never be the same. He told me the humane thing to do was to let her go. She was under anesthesia, she was not in any pain and she would go peacefully. I waited for her father to get there and we went in to say our goodbyes.

It was the hardest thing I've ever done in my life. My Angel had saved my life but I could not save hers. I cried and I held her as she lay there with all of the tubes coming out of her body. Crying, the same as I am crying now as I write her story. REM REM my sweet Remi, I love you, you are going to a better place, a place where you can play all the time, and chase bees, and squirrels and eat everything you want. I will always be with you. I will always love you. I kissed her snout and I hugged her as tight as I could and I let her go. I lost my child that night. No one can ever tell me any different. She was not a dog. She was a living breathing soul and to this day I miss her and I feel her. She was and is my angel.

My father blamed himself, and I blamed myself for her death, but now I believe God took Remi because it was her time. And Remi knew that it was too hard for me to take care of myself, my father and my three girls; so she knew she could look out for us better on the other side. I spoke of that distinctive smell she had, maybe it was the smell of an angel. Remi was my Angel here on earth and she now looks out for us up above. Every now and then I smell that smell. Sydney and Georgia smell it too and they go right to the cabinet where her ashes and collar are displayed with her pictures and we all just take a moment, or sometimes we howl a song.

My father's walking now. But there's something funny about the novena candles I would burn for him to get well… The ash on the glass would take the shape of a wolf or a dog. That may sound strange to most, but I believe in Angels, and I know that we have one more looking out for us now. And her name is REM REM.

REM REM brought me and everyone who knew her seven years of insurmountable joy. Her death brought me pain and sadness, which I can only describe as losing a child. I wish that she was not taken from us so soon, but God has a plan. I am grateful for the time that I had with my baby, and because of her I still exist. I know that she continues to look after us here on earth. I believe also that she resides in heaven with the rest of my family, they take care of her now, or perhaps she takes care of them, and brings joy to them with her crazy antics. I know that she is waiting for me and the rest of her family to join her in paradise.

Now, as I fight back the tears it is time to move on; time to tell the story of my Sweetie Pie, My Old Girl, The Queen, Mouth Almighty, Smiley, Secret Squirrel. Yes, it's time for the story of my gorgeous, oldest, and first little girl, Georgia.

5

GEORGIA

G EORGIA was born on May 12, 1996; six days after my Mother had passed away.

When I was a child I had always wanted a dog, I was never one to play with dolls, I had my Lassie and every other stuffed animal imaginable they were my friends. Growing up as an only child is hard especially when your mother is ill, you grow up quickly in some ways and in others you remain a child at heart one with an incredible imagination. My stuffed animals were my babies and I begged for a real dog or pet but because of my mother's condition and my allergies I was unable to have one. I would continue to play with my stuffed toys and hope that someday I would have a pet, I would sleep with them all surrounding me, kind of how I sleep with my girls now around my head below my feet, a circle of stuffed animals all around me to keep me safe from the world.

I lived with my grandparents, aunt and cousins for a little while, when my mother was hospitalized and my father couldn't take care of me; I was about five. They had two poodles and I was extremely allergic to them. My eyes would close shut and itch as I got older. I had an allergy test done which said that I had both dog and cat allergies. I knew I had horrible cat allergies; my reaction was so bad my throat would close up. I always prayed that I would grow out of it, but I didn't know if I ever would.

My mother had severe rheumatoid arthritis and osteoporosis, which caused her bones to be so brittle that the smallest fall could turn into a most severe break. So she had an ongoing fear of animals; although she loved them, she was always afraid of tripping over them.

Because of these two very distinct reasons, while growing up I was unable to have a pet except for my funny little gold fishes, which were cute. I remember having our funerals in the backyard for my little Goldie, Goldie 2, Spottie and Stripes. My mother and I buried so many shoeboxes in that backyard when I was a child. She would tell me, "They all went to the big aquarium in heaven".

I still yearned for my dog. You know, man's (or in this case woman's) best friend; and I finally found her. And my first little girl could not have come at a time more needed; after the death of my best friend, the death of my mother. Sometimes I think that with her stubbornness she is my mother reincarnated. Georgia is definitely a dog of personality. I must take into account she is a four-legged person with a mouth on her that could summon the dead. She will let you know exactly what she thinks of you in a heartbeat, and in many ways she is cat like.

My husband and I had been married about a year; we were living in an apartment and house hunting. My mother had passed away about a month earlier. I was going through a very difficult time; dealing with the loss of my mother, and helping my father, who was extremely depressed and looking for a new home. I needed something desperately to come into my life. This really wasn't the good life for a newlywed. I had only been married a year.

Kellianne M. Peterson

My husband was shopping one afternoon at the Home Depot and I happened to walk outside for a cigarette. Next door was a puppy store. I decided to go in just to play with the dogs. I knew it was a reputable pet store because I knew people who had gotten their puppies there. I also knew that the owners would take home any of the dogs that were not sold and keep them so they would not end up homeless. I knew they were decent people, and good to the dogs - not like some of the "bad" pet store owners you hear about on the news.

I went into the store. I was petting the pups, playing with all of them. They were all so adorable. Then out of the corner of my eye, in the last crate, there were three tiny little pups. Two were vying for my attention and one was curled up in a little white ball. I went over to the three of them and she looked up at me; the most precious little thing, this little white snowball with the black coal eyes staring back at me. The moment I saw her I fell in love with her, her silky long white hair and those ebony eyes with a little pink nose and black rimmed mouth. She was a timid little thing, shaking in the corner of the pen she was in. I asked the storekeeper, "How old is she?" She replied, "She is six weeks old; a pure bred American Eskimo." I had never heard of an American Eskimo dog before. She told me, "They are in the Spitz family, and they are sort of a miniature Samoyed or a large Pomeranian." Now I knew that Samoyed were big, nervous dogs with a lot of hair (allergies!) and I always loved Pomeranians so I was at a crossroads. I kept petting her in the crate. She was just so cute, and she kept looking up at me as if she was trying to figure me out. "Who is this strange person?" She probably was thinking, "Why is she petting me, why is she talking baby talk to me? She is such a weirdo…"

My husband finally came into the shop, and he saw me with her. I said, "I think I want to get her but she is so shy." My husband said, "If she is going to be this shy and timid she might not take to us, or she might be a nipper." My husband didn't like little dogs; he was always afraid that they would nip. But I was already so taken with her. The storekeeper suggested we bring her into the playroom and see if she would go to either of us. We went into the playroom; she was extremely shy and coy at first. I rolled a ball to her, she looked at it, and stood there shuddering. I rolled it to her again very slowly. I kept smiling at her, "Come on girl, come on honey you can do it, play with the ball." She looked at the ball, she looked at me and she scurried across the floor, right into my arms and that was the first time she smiled and she started licking my face. She loved me and I found my new best friend. I found my first baby, my first little girl. I found my little Angel.

I was afraid the car ride might be a disaster on our first day home, but my little girl proved to be the Angel I thought that she was. I held her in my lap as my husband drove and then I started to hear this tiny little sound coming from my lap. My little girl was purring. She was so content in her new Mommy's lap that she just lay there purring away. Occasionally she would lick my hand or look up at me and smile; she was content and so was I.

Before we took her home, her first stop was at my Dad's. I wanted him to see how happy I was now that I found my little Angel. We knocked on his door. I carried her like a baby, and she was so tiny. My father opened the door, and he was taken back. The first thing she did when we put her down was to piddle on the rug because she was so nervous. And she cried because she piddled. My father was not happy that she piddled and he was worried that we would be thrown out of our apartment but he took to her. I could tell because he started to pick on her. That is how my father shows his love; he needles and teases a lot like my ex-husband. Who says girls don't marry their fathers? Unfortunately it doesn't always work out.

My father put out some water for her but she wouldn't go into the kitchen to drink it. We tried cereal, then we tried milk; aha, that spiked her interest. She kept stretching her head to try to get to the milk but she wouldn't walk on the kitchen floor. The kitchen floor was tile. She was afraid to walk on the tile floor so we had to move the milk closer to her so she could drink it. Drink she did, she loved her milk and after she was done she would lick her paws clean like a cat. Yes, that was her thing. She loved her milk and she always would keep herself clean and as she would get older her aloofness would prove to be more a cat like than my other two girls.

Next we had to decide on a name, we went through the obvious names of Frosty, Snowball, Crystal, Baby, Princess (which would have fit her just fine) and a half a dozen other typical dog names. After all she was my first, but my husband had grown up with dogs. Oh, we went through so many, and then we had a thought during the summer Olympics. One of my best friends lives in Georgia. Hmmmm! "Georgia, come here Georgia." I said. She looked up, smiled and scampered over to me. That is how she got her name. "Sweet Georgia Brown" a song I used to ice dance to as a teenager or "Georgie Girl" a song I used to sing as a child. All pleasant memories to me, and the name fit her. It wasn't till years later that I also remembered a promise that I had made to myself when I was in my early twenties that I was going to name my first dog GG after my friend George when he had been shot. Thank God he survived, alive and well with a child of his own now, but kind of weird she didn't end up with the name GG. But she did end up with the name Georgia. Funny how things turn out; she was meant to be a George.

We left my father's and went home. The next task at hand was putting together the crate. As everyone knows, and from what I was told, the first step to housebreaking a dog is crate training. Now I'm not going to go make a step by step chapter on how to crate train your dog, but I will tell you that Georgia was the easiest dog to housebreak and to this day as she approaches her 11 birthday it is a rarity that she will mess in the house. However, if she does, expect a flood and an extremely indignant attitude if it was your fault or tears of embarrassment if it was her fault.

When we brought Georgia home the first night my husband put together her crate and we played with her. She loved to play tug-o-war; she loved her ropey toys and anything she could chew on. She wasn't much for balls or the run and go fetch thing. After playing, it was time to go to sleep, so we put her in the crate with one of my t-shirts and newspapers down the other end in case she needed to go during the night, and went to bed. She was so good; barely a whimper, and she went to sleep.

That was the end of our first day with Georgia.

The next morning, my husband got up and walked her around outside the front of our apartment. She was afraid to go to the bathroom; she would keep walking around and around looking for a spot to go. My husband finally gave up. "You take her out when you get ready for work, I have to leave," he bellowed. He put her back in the crate. My husband wasn't a very patient man.

I got out of the shower a little bit later. Georgia was whimpering in her crate; she had gone to the bathroom in her crate and she didn't like it. It was okay, she had gone on the newspaper but that was the way she was, she did not like to mess and she was cowering in the corner of the crate with my tee shirt and her toy.

All and all it took Georgia a total of three days to be completely housebroken and crate trained. We kept the crate intact until we moved into our new house "just in case" for those times that we were both out, but she never messed in it again. She actually felt safe in it with her toys and my t-shirt when we weren't home.

Georgia only messed two times in that apartment; and it was my fault. I was getting ready for work one morning and she kept pacing and pacing around me I kept telling her "hold on Georgia, one minute." Well the poor little girl couldn't wait one more minute and she had a bowel movement. She looked at me her eyes welled up with tears and she just started crying, looking at me as if to say, "I tried to tell you Mom."

The other time, I was on the phone talking to one of my girlfriends and she had just been out for a walk and she didn't go. Well, she started her little dance, walking around looking at me while I was on the phone; the next thing I know she got this look on her face, looked directly at me, squatted and took a pee right in front of me. That is when I learned my little Sweet Georgie Girl had a defiant, spiteful side. Not to mention a mouth! I jumped off the phone grabbed her and her leash, and took her outside so she could finish her business. I brought her back inside, showed her where she messed, told her "No," and what did my sweet little Georgia do? She stamped her front two paws and started barking at me. I was dumb-founded. My dog was having a temper tantrum. After she was finished with her little display she went into her crate and sulked. I did not tell her to go into her crate as a punishment. She went in on her own; she thought she was punishing me. Interesting! This was not a one-time occurrence between Georgia and I, as our mother and daughter power struggles still go on. The temper tantrums have mellowed but the stubbornness, mouth, sulking, and moodiness live on.

Yes, Georgia was the easiest to housebreak indeed, but she is the most stubborn and aloof of my four legged children. She has her human side too. She definitely was her mother's daughter and she did not want to be held as you would hold a dog; she wanted to be held as you would hold a baby. She still would piddle from time to time when she was scared or excited. Unfortunately it would usually be on the person she was scared or excited about, which brings to mind two stories.

I was a day manager and bartender at a local bar when Georgia came into our lives. Sometimes my husband would come up to the bar for a drink after he was done work or in some cases to pick me up if I didn't drive in that day. Everyone in the bar knew that I had just gotten a new puppy, and being the proud mother that I was I had tons of pictures, but they didn't do my Sweetie Pie justice. This one particular day I didn't drive to work and I was waiting for my husband to come pick me up, the door opens and everyone says, "Look here comes your little girl" "She's so adorable." Well, adorable she was, and petrified she was. Then she saw me sitting there at the bar with some patrons and it was all that she could do to wiggle free from her father. Not making a sound paws out in front, scrambling for her mommy, trying to reach for me like a baby does when they want their mommy or daddy. I finally took her from her father and held her like a mother would, and she peed right down the front of my shirt! She was so scared and excited. My poor little girl was trembling, and then she started to whimper and buried her head in my neck. She hated when she tinkled and people saw it; she was very private about that and she still is to this day.

Another favorite "Georgia bar story" involved me being the day manger, which meant part of my duties was to train the new girls. I would go in on my day off for an hour or two, open the bar, get them set up, show them the ropes and make sure everything was running smooth before I would leave. But I didn't like to leave Georgia on my days off. She was so little; she would give me this look and I would feel so sorry for her. I decided to take her with me one morning. How hard could it be? She'll just walk around the bar or lay there while I do what I have to do, right? Wrong! The minute she couldn't see me she would cry, so I thought I'd move her behind the bar where she could see me. Wrong again! She didn't like the rubber mats on the floor. Okay, I'll sit her on top of the bar, so she can see everywhere I go; she will just lie there, and there's no mat so she won't fall into the little holes. Not happening. My little girl wanted to be carried! Remember, Georgia is not a dog; she is a four-legged little baby who has temper tantrums and cries. So I picked her up and she wrapped her front paws around my neck, her hind paws around my waist, and I scooched her to my side so I could rest her on my hip like a mother walks around holding her child. And I went about my work. She was happy then, but I had an aching back by the time we left.

Our first couple of months with Georgia was an extremely endearing learning experience. She loved to play and chew; I lost so many pairs of shoe strings that month. Her favorites were my favorite Wolverine Work boots. They were under constant replacement.

She would constantly drag them around and they became her favorite toy. We also found out that she was a prankster and she was quick. My husband took her out one morning to do her business and he was very lax with her lead because she was so obedient. Well this particular morning she had the devil in her. She took off, and while she was running she kept turning around with this big grin on her face as if to say, "Go ahead you can't catch me." Luckily my husband was able to catch her because she always has to stop, sniff and mark. I think she gets a little distracted from her running because something will catch her eye that she just has to investigate, which will give you enough time to sneak up and get her, but you've got to be quick or she's off again, laughing at you all the way!

6

OUR MOVE TO OUR NEW

HOUSE

The end of September 1996 we began moving in to our new house. It was a cute little house in New Jersey, just big enough for the three of us; Georgia, my husband and me. Our first day of moving in was a little traumatic for our little girl; she sniffed around the house and she loved exploring the new back yard that she had to play in, and to my delight it was fenced in. Then it happened, I was downstairs checking out the basement, my husband was outside loading more stuff into the garage and Georgia was in the living room by herself. It was hot that year and there wasn't any furniture in the house yet. Of course she was afraid to walk on the kitchen floor that would lead to the basement so she couldn't look to see if I was downstairs. She had never even been in a place with stairs before. The next thing I heard was her weeping. I ran upstairs; she was sitting in the middle of the living room shaking and whimpering amidst her mess. She thought that she had been abandoned, and got the diarrhea all over the living room, mostly by the door way and the windows. She was looking for a way to get out. I felt so bad for my little girl, I couldn't yell at her. She was so frightened. I just picked her up, hugged her and kissed her tears away.

Once we were moved in Georgia became quite settled and loved the new house except for the basement and for the stairs. It took her months to go up the stairs to the master bedroom, and I don't think in the three years that we lived in that house did she ever venture into the basement. But the backyard was her domain. She would patrol that yard like a guard on duty. She showed her skills as a watchdog much to the dismay of our neighbors. Georgia would walk the edge of the fence and bark at each point of intersection as if to say, "This is my property, I'm on duty! I protect my family and my home." That's when she became nick named Mouth Almighty because an Almighty Mouth and bark she did have. Yes, her mouth, and that bark of hers became one of the reasons we eventually moved from our first house in that small New Jersey town. That, and because even though we abided by all the local dog laws and noise regulations, some of the neighbors insisted on calling the cops who considered her a nuisance. These people were definitely not animal lovers and as we found out later they had complained about every dog in the neighborhood.

Sweetie Pie loved our new home but she was horrified of the stairs. I awoke one night to this scratching sound; I didn't understand what it was. I crept downstairs worried that someone was trying to break in, and worried about Georgie because she still did not come upstairs. But there she was chewing on the bottom step, scraping, chewing and sharpening her chops on the bottom landing. Yes she was a weird one. After that I carried her to bed at night to make sure she wouldn't get into more trouble, or try any more artistic endeavors with the stairs. Yes, I guess she was part beaver, as well as human and cat.

One of her most favorite things to do was jump up on the couch, sit in the window, watch everything go by and of course, bark. She also loved to eat burritos and tacos from Taco Bell or pretty much anything that was in my hand. I would sit on the floor or the couch and she would sit above and to the side of me and eat over my shoulder she did this until she was about a year old, and she was a picky little thing too. God forbid you gave the little princess a nacho without cheese on it or a pretzel without mustard. Yes, I spoiled her rotten but she was my first-born. LOL.

The Queen would go everywhere with me, I could take her almost everywhere that would allow me to because she was so well behaved and she loved driving in the car. Georgia would just sit in the front seat and look out the window and watch everyone. She would love to go to the bank because she knew she was always going to get a treat and they would make a fuss over how pretty her coat was and say "My God what a happy dog, she's smiling at me." And she was definitely smiling.

Her most favorite place to go in the world was Pet Smart. She hated the floors mind you, so I would pick her up and let her ride in the cart. She was the bell of the ball, and at Christmas time, she would go see Santa. She knew she was Ms. Thing and she would strut her stuff and sniff out what she wanted for Christmas. There never was a bad picture of Georgia ever taken. To this day Georgia is a ham for the camera.

7

GEORGIA & THE VETS

When we first brought Georgia home we were assigned a Vet to take her to for her shots, and that is where we went. He seemed nice enough and knowledgeable. The first time we went for her shots Georgia seemed a little leery. I know that is where the pet shop recommended that she go but she didn't seem pleased; but then what child or puppy would be? She was getting shots.

The second time she went was when she had to get fixed, which was a horrible experience for me, and my poor little girl. She had a little problem with the anesthesia and they almost didn't let her come home. When they finally did she was not feeling well that night, if you know what I mean.

The third and last time we took her to that vet he checked her incision, administered her last round of shots and then he started looking around her butt and checking her hind legs. I had told him she had been wobbly lately. He explained, "That she was having a growth spurt and was possibly having some knee/hip problems, and just to keep an eye on it and give her baby aspirin for the inflammation and pain." Well, sweetie pie had enough with him nosing around her butt and turned around and snapped at him. She didn't actually try to bite him but she showed her teeth and growled.

From that point on she did not like anyone around her butt. She also became extremely particular about who her vet was, and a female vet was a definite requirement. If she saw a male vet she would get very shy, and if they tried to get near her for an exam forget it. It was just not happening.

Once we moved, the search for a new vet was on, we finally found a very nice female vet. Yes, Georgia still needs to be muzzled for her shots especially if you get to close to her butt; however, at least she is a lot happier and will permit examinations. She even enjoys getting up on the scale, but my God if there is a male replacement that day all hell breaks loose. Unfortunately, I guess she will always have that childhood trauma from her first veterinary experience.

Thank God she isn't scared of the groomer. They are usually female, so I shouldn't say she isn't fearful, but when she is first dropped off she doesn't want to go in. They have to coax her, but she never cries, and she obediently goes. But when I pick her up she is happy and she knows she is the cat's meow. She struts around like a show dog, enjoying her treats from the Groomer and all the attention she gets from everyone who tells her how pretty she looks. She wags her tail, smiles, sits in the front seat of the car and takes in the view like she is the Queen of the Ball. I swear if she could wave at the people going by she would say "Look at me! Look at Me!" I'm so pretty!" Smiling ear to ear, yes going to the groomer is one of her favorite things. There was only one groomer she didn't like going to, and like that vet we stopped going to. You have to listen to your animals; they usually have their reasons. Maybe they are neglected there, or the person

is too rough with them; but they have their reasons,

same as we do for switching doctors or hairdressers; I'll

say it again; they are four-legged little people.

My Angels, My Girls

8

GEORGIA GETS A SISTER

My sweetie-pie needed a sister. She needed someone to play with, and my husband said that Georgia was too much a Mommy's girl and he wanted a dog of his own. Georgia and I went to the pet shop one day where we got her and we were playing with a beautiful Australian Shepherd. He was so adorable, but too docile. Georgia scared the daylights out of him so that was the end of that. I thought to myself, "Maybe Georgia wants to be an only child." Well, my husband still wanted his big dog, one that he could train and that would listen to him. Georgia only listened to me, and then sometimes she would give me an argument, and stamp her paws, but she would never mess in the house. Although she would eat the comforter, the pillows, and make artistic tooth designs on the stairs and many shoes that had to be replaced, she was a good dog - just temperamental and prissy.

My husband and I went back to the store and we looked around. I had wanted to go to the shelter, but he wanted a puppy that he could train so we looked; and I was looking at dogs that were around Georgia's size. My husband was like, "No I want a big dog." Then we saw her laying there curled up sleeping. We went over and he said "That's her. I want her. A big Siberian Husky." She was certainly the biggest dog in the store and she was only six weeks old. Then she opened up her eyes. She had the most beautiful eyes I had ever seen; big and blue, and she had the same

birthday as my mother who had passed away two years
before January 26, 1998. My mother had died on May
6, 1996. She was really cute but she had this smell. I
thought," Wow! I hope she doesn't have that animal
dander that I am allergic to." Plus her coat was so thick
and Huskies shed like crazy. Georgia's hair was more
like human hair; long and silky not like a dog. Then my
husband picked her up, and she kissed him. And then
she looked at me and gave this little cry like she was
trying to talk. Like she was trying to say, "Please take
me home." What could I do? I said to my husband
"Okay, but I get to name her! You named Georgia."
So, she was christened Remi and everyone thought she
was named after the alcohol, but actually she was
named after a cop on a TV show called the "Big Easy"
that I had a silly crush on at the time. She lived up to

her name of Remi relating to the alcohol; however, she took after her father that way.

We drove home from the pet store with Remi sitting on my lap crying like a baby. Unlike Georgia she did not like the car. I tried to keep her calm as she was squirming all over me, beating me up, howling, talking and crawling all over me. I thought it was not going to work. We got home and walked through the door; me, my husband, and our new bundle of joy. Well, Georgia was needless to say, not pleased.

Georgia looked at Remi, sniffed her and barked. Remi looked at Georgia and talked. This went on for about an hour. As the night went on, my husband set up the crate again for Remi as we did with Georgie. They kept their distance from each other slowly sniffing each other, barking and talking getting the feel for one another. At this point in time they were the same size; perhaps Georgia was actually a little bigger than REM REM, as she would soon be called. The crate was finally set up and it was time to go to sleep. We put Remi in the crate and went up to bed, my husband, my Georgia and me. Remi was left downstairs in the living room in the crate. In the middle of the night, I heard this howling and crying. Remi was up and Georgia was by her crate clawing at it. I don't know which started first; maybe Remi was crying and Georgia went down to see if she was okay, or maybe Georgia went down and woke her up as if to say, "You're in there and I'm out here." "I sleep with Mommy and Daddy, and you sleep in there." I don't know what the situation was, but I ended up staying down there until she went to sleep and Georgia decided to sleep by her on the floor next to the crate.

The next day after we let them both out in the yard they started to warm up to each other. They would play and run after each other. It seems so funny looking back both of them being the same size at that time; it would only take a few months before Remi would tower over Georgia. Georgia would jump on the couch and lay there and Remi would try to crawl up on the couch and smack Georgia. She was always smacking Georgia when she was on the couch as if she was saying, "Hey I want to be up there too." Or, "Get down here with me." It was a hilarious sight to see, something I will always remember and cherish.

Oh, Remi hated being in that crate at night. She would howl and cry. When she had to go in while we were at work we would come home to the crate completely torn apart. Georgia sitting there smiling this little smug smile and Remi happy that I came home. I think Georgia tormented her during the day; teasing her that she was stuck in her cage and that she had the freedom to roam the house. Unfortunately the crate did not last very long in our house with Remi. We felt so sorry for her and we paid the price. It took a very long time to housebreak her but at least she was able to play with Georgia and be happy while we were at work. Georgia couldn't tease her anymore. She eventually learned how to jump on the couch and climb the steps, and soon they both were sleeping in the bedroom with my husband and me.

Georgia and Remi eventually became like typical sisters; they would fight like sisters, but they would stick up for each other too. Georgia even taught Remi how to talk back to her mother and stamp her paws, so now I had two of them. The difference between them; however, was Georgia had this stubborn, moody streak and Remi always aimed to please.

The two little sisters became like Frick and Frack and they would follow each other all around. Georgia would take the lead even as Remi grew. One day as I was pulling up in the car with them both inside, we were coming back from a visit with my dad or something; Georgia of course had been sitting in the front seat enjoying the ride as always. Remi had been crying and carrying on the whole time; I opened the car door and Georgia jumped out along with Remi and I tripped, and they both got away from me. They both ran up the street. I called for them, and Georgia looked back at me laughing, Remi would stop but then she would see Georgia still running so she would keep on going after her. Thankfully, a neighbor grabbed that little white trickster and as soon as she was contained

Remi heeled. I yelled at them all the way home. Remi walked along side of me head and tail hung low she knew she was in trouble and that she shouldn't have run. Georgia stubbornly sat down and wouldn't budge with this defiant look on her face. Oh she was something. I embarrassed her in public by yelling at her. My God what an insult. I had to carry her home. My spoiled little queen! I had to pick her up like a child and carry her all the way home as she pouted.

Georgia never liked to be reprimanded. She is the sweetest, well behaved, loving dog and as she got older and our family grew I think she felt a little bit left out of the limelight. She was Mommy's first and was the baby for the first two years. Yes, sometimes I feel that she doesn't feel as though she gets the attention she used to get, but she is always loved and she still sleeps with me every night. Reprimand her, and she will pout and never admit she is wrong.

Remi and Georgia were playing in the backyard one day, and all of sudden I heard this growling and squealing. I thought they were fighting with each other, but no, they had gotten a hold of a baby bunny. I was mortified. They were tugging at it and pulling at it. I never thought of my dogs as killers but it is their natural instinct to hunt, and the rabbits had been getting in our yard and eating our vegetables, and flowers. They thought they were protecting their home. I on the other hand was hysterical. The poor bunny! I ripped it from their grip. I smacked them both on the snout and on their butts. I was yelling at them, looking at the poor dead bunny, worried about what diseases they could have gotten from the bunny. Wondering if the taste of live blood would change them; make them wild. God did the bunny have rabies or something else? All kinds of terrible thoughts flew through my mind. I was so angry with them for what they did. I didn't raise them to be predatory. Yet, it's in every dog's nature to hunt and protect. These two are usually so gentle; they play with every other dog and cat. What got into them? I just had to hope for the best, but I had to make sure they didn't do it again. I pulled them both over to the dead bunny pointed to it and told them, "NO!" I spanked their behinds and put them in the garage. I never spanked them before and I wanted them to know what they had done was very bad; especially the way they had ripped it apart like a rag doll. Fifteen minutes didn't go by before Remi was whimpering and scratching at the door. I opened the door and she kissed my face and lowered her tail to show that she knew she had done wrong and was sorry.

I looked over at Georgia; I said "Are you ready to come in Georgie?" "Are you sorry?" Do you know what she did? Georgia stuck her nose up in the air, turned her back to me and looked at the wall. I said, "Come on Georgia. Come in the house." Remi even went over to her and howled at her to come in. But that stubborn little girl sat in that garage staring at the wall until her father came home two hours later. She then hugged and kissed him to his surprise and ignored me the rest of the night. Georgia did not like to be reprimanded.

9

GEORGIA & HER DADDY

Georgia did have a special relationship with her father when he would come in at night because he eventually went on shift work. He would call her his "Secret Squirrel" because she would love to play hide and seek with him. He would come home at night play with the others and she would hide. I would hear him. "Where's my Secret Squirrel?" "Where's my little Squirrelly Squirrel?" I would then hear her scampering about and barking, making this little growl she makes when she would play. They were happy times for all of us especially for him and Georgia. They were really special to my little girl. She doesn't play too much anymore but I'm sure she remembers her "Secret Squirrel" days.

She still likes to play hide and seek only now she does it in my bed. Like a little gopher she burrows through the blankets and comes up underneath the pillows right up to my face and plants a big kiss on me, or starts breathing on me through that big smile of hers that she has had since she was a pup. My sweet Georgia Brown may be getting up in age but she is still my little Angel.

10

MOVING TIME AGAIN:

THE BIG HOUSE

Georgia was about three and a half and Remi was about one and a half and we were outgrowing our small cape cod. With Remi growing at such a rapid pace we were also outgrowing the nastiness of the couple next door who constantly complained about our little Mouth Almighty. Even though we adhered to the township guidelines they were constantly complaining. We also feared for the safety of our little ones when we started to find things in our yard and one of the other dogs that were complained about turned up missing. We knew it was time to move.

I also at that time wanted to move my father in with us even though he was quite self sufficient. I didn't like the fact that he was living alone anymore in another state. With all of our money pooled together we were able to afford a beautiful house with a yard three times the size of what we had in our small town. One problem; there wasn't a fence at our new house and I wanted a privacy fence to curtail Mouth Almighty's barking. My logic was, if she couldn't see it - she couldn't bark at it. Well that did not turn out to be true but luckily in this new neighborhood everyone was a dog lover and loved my girls, so there weren't any problems. However, there was the problem of the three weeks with no fence at all.

The day we moved in, Georgia and Remi explored the house from top to bottom. They were amazed at its size. Remi ran all over it, up and down the stairs all over it top to bottom. Georgia on the other hand; the kitchen floor had to be investigated, bathroom floors, sniffed but not ventured into. She slowly edged her way upstairs and inspected each bedroom and closet. The basement, no sir! She looked at those stairs, turned right back around and let out a big "Huh, I'm not going down there, don't want to, can't make me try it. NO WAY!" Then they both saw the backyard. Their eyes lit up like they had a slice of heaven before them - green grass and trees like they never saw before and no boundaries holding them in. Then they both looked down and saw two leashes with chains they were horrified.

I never used to tie Georgia and Remi up. I had to tie Remi up once when she got loose, but she broke it anyway. Then I didn't do it again and she never ran away again because she got scared. But Georgia, she had never been on a tie in her life. She looked at me with these eyes of disdain, and Remi almost the same way, but Remi was getting ready to enter her terrible twos soon. She was a year and half old and I was a bit frightened of what she may do.

The first day they were on that tie my fears were correct. Georgia wiggled her head out of her collar and Remi broke the chain. They both run amuck through our new neighborhood. Remi was six yards down jumping fences like a gazelle when my husband finally caught up to her. Georgia was nowhere to be found. Finally, she comes strolling down the back lawn; not a care in the world and just lays down in the yard, looking at me as if to say, "What? You think I can't find my own way home Mommy? I'm a big girl I was just out exploring and I don't like that collar. Why are you worried?" Yes, my little princess was growing up. She lay there in the grass with her paws crossed in front of her. The little poser; ready for a photo shoot and telling me by her actions she was all grown up and ready to take on the world - but she was still Mommy's little girl.

The fence soon went up and Georgia now had a bigger area to patrol; and patrol she did, my little sentry would, as soon as she would go out of the back sliding glass doors from the family room. She would look right, then left, march down the steps of the deck and immediately go over to the fence and start her daily routine tracing the perimeter of the fence, letting out a bark at each corner, making her presence known to the world. Georgia would then find a place to do her business, her own private place; and if she caught you watching she would let out an annoyed huff and find another. Georgia was always private about those things as most little ladies are.

Yes, the girls loved the new house; more rooms to roam around in and a big yard to play in. They were both happy as larks. Georgia was especially happy. She had more rooms to hide in. Secret Squirrel was especially happy to be able to play hide and seek with her father. She also was happy that her grandfather was living with us too. She was the center of attention again. Her pop-pop was there and he always gave her cookies, treats and spoiled her. She was the first grand-puppy. He still babied her. Mommy and daddy were always working. They had time at night and on the weekends, but grandpa was there all day long and he spoiled Georgia and Remi rotten. It was a happy time for all.

Georgia and Remi would go to see Santa and Santa would make all their Christmas dreams come true three times over. The girls, believe it or not, would not touch their stockings before Christmas; they would sniff them, but never touch them. Come Christmas it was a free for all; they would open their gifts, tear them apart and there would be wrapping paper and doggy treats and toys all over the living room. I didn't care; after all they were my children.

Springtime and summertime should have been renamed "The Shedding Time" around our house. Georgia would shed, but Remi, you could stuff a pillow or comforter. Plus, with the heat we had heard that you should shave your dogs. I found out later that this wasn't a good practice to do and that dogs never should be shaved. Their fur actually helps with heating and cooling, but at that time that was the practice we followed. Georgia and Remi were the funniest looking dogs I ever saw. Georgia looked like a larger Taco Bell dog and Remi; she must have wanted to kill us. She was shaved everywhere except her face. It looked like a little tiny squared off lion head and she had a tiny pom pom at the tip of her tail with a bow. I don't know what the groomers were thinking especially with REM REM but we kept telling them how adorable they looked and Georgia actually did look really cute, but poor Remi! The different styles these groomers would give her; what were they thinking? I just look back at the pictures now and laugh.

Summertime brought another new thing of exploration for the girls and a major pain for me. We had a beautiful deck off the back of our new house.

Well Georgia and Remi had decided that underneath the deck would make a wonderful fort to get away from the sun or the rain; so they would borough little holes under the deck. The problem was Remi would come out from under the deck when she was called. Georgia being Georgia would not come out and you would have to crawl under the deck to get her.

One summer night, there was this thunderstorm which came up suddenly and Georgia ran underneath the deck, scared to death. She went so far under I couldn't reach her. I tried to coax her out with treats, then the broom. She was just cowering in the center, all the way to the back, closest to the house, in a hole covered with mud, whimpering. I finally had to get on my belly and crawl under the deck all the way to where she was and pull her out, and she did not want to come. After about a half hour of dragging and pulling she finally surrendered and let me take her out from underneath the deck. We both emerged soaked and covered with mud, but safe, and the thunderstorm was over

Georgia always hated thunderstorms and to this day she will hide, or she has to be with her Mommy. Remi didn't particularly like thunderstorms either, but her way of dealing with them was to sit on my bed and howl at them.

11

GEORGIA & REMI GET

ANOTHER SISTER

L ike most families you encounter rough patches. Our family was not immune to such patches, and unfortunately this one rough patch would turn into a gaping hole, but it would also bring another little gift of love into our lives.

We had been living in our house for about a year, and my husband and I had been trying to have a baby unsuccessfully for years. This had put a lot of strain on our marriage among other problems, which was causing it to slowly disintegrate. Like a lot of people trying to save their marriage with a child, we tried to save our marriage with another puppy.

The day we brought Sydney home, no one was happy. My father said "Another one? You're crazy!" and proceeded to throw up his hands in disgust. Remi was not a happy camper and ended up biting her on the ear that night to show her that she was not going to be pushed aside by some little runt. My little Sweetie Pie Georgia just looked at me with disgust. She had this look of loathing directed toward her Mommy as if she was asking, "How could you do this to me again?"

My husband and I thought this would help us and bring us closer together. Of course like so many other people that try this with a baby, it didn't, we eventually separated and divorced years later. The girls on the other hand became a force to be reckoned with;

they became a little pack. **Georgia the matriarch, Remi the leader, and Sydney the baby.** They would play together; well Remi and Sydney would play. Georgia would lie there with her paws crossed and observe. They would stick up for each other and like human sisters, they would fight, but they would never hurt each other physically. But they did play psychological war games on each other.

One of the funniest things would be the food stare down, which went something like this. They all loved spaghetti & meatballs, or roast beef, so I would make up three plates for them and put them out on the floor. I would put Georgia's out first so she could get a head start because she ate very slowly. Remi and Sydney practically inhaled their food. After Remi and Sydney were done they would stare Georgia down because she would still be eating. Sydney being a little sneak, and still a baby would try to find ways to sneak the food off of Georgia's plate, which would end up with Georgia growling at her but not snapping - just enough to scare her. But Remi would just stare her down until Georgia would finally walk away. Remi would never touch her food, but she would just stare her down until Georgia finally would be like, "Okay already." Then the food would be gone in a flash and Sydney wouldn't even get a scrap, and she would look at Remi. "Thanks a lot, you forgot about me." Remi would slink away and look back at her and I swear she was snickering. I think Remi had a little bit of middle child syndrome and Georgia definitely had that first child power she held over them all. Sydney was the baby all the way.

In April 2002, I had my first stroke, I had my heart surgery in May, my husband moved out that June and I had my second stroke in August 2002. This was a trying time for my little brood. Georgia was now almost six years old, Remi was four, and Sydney was almost two. Georgia would lie beside my bed when I came home from my first stroke, or if someone would put her in the bed with me she would lay next to me in bed. She would mostly just look at me and smile, or come over and kiss my hand. Georgia pretty much took a back seat during my illness and let Remi run the show. Sometimes I think she knew that REM REM was stronger and able to protect me better, so she would just sit back watch, pray, and observe. She did have the honor of being the one to bring me home from the rehabilitation center after my second stroke. They gave her that and she was proud, sitting in the car and helping me with my cane; walking along side of me when I got home. I had been away for what seemed to be forever.

It was rough for me after I came home from rehab. There was a lot of residual effects from the stroke. The physical therapy and rehabilitation I received helped immensely, but I had a long road ahead of me. My girls, their antics, the trouble they would get into, their hilarious moments and constant companionship, love and protection gave me the will and strength to go on.

Georgia was funny. Of course Remi the championship talker never would bark, she would only talk or howl and Sydney being a Siberian Husky didn't know how to howl. Well Remi decided this wasn't going to fly. She was going to teach Sydney how to howl. One night we are all sitting on my bed, Remi starts howling, Sydney, starts barking, Remi howls at her in a scolding way; I start howling trying to help Sydney learn. We are finally all howling, and then I hear this little combo-bark-howl. Georgia starts trying to howl and join in. American Eskimos don't howl but she was doing it. She was part of the pack and she was going to learn how to howl with the rest of us. From that night on as much as it drove my father bonkers and probably my neighbors we had our little howl-fests. Sydney eventually learned and Georgia would do her little combo and Remi was happy she had her pack in check.

My Angels, My Girls

12

MY FIRST SCARE

Times continued to have their ups and downs, then for me one of my fears became a reality. One of my children was sick. I noticed that Georgia was playing less and less, and gaining a lot of weight. I took Georgia to the vet and they said that she may have Cushing Syndrome or Hypothyroid, but considering her symptoms it really looked like Cushing. Georgia was only about seven years old. For her to be diagnosed with Cushing this young I was devastated. My poor little angel! Once again, I prayed to God, to Jesus, the Blessed Mother; I made offerings to the

Saints, I prayed to Saint Francis of Assisi, and Saint Lazarus. I hadn't prayed so much since my mother was sick, and when Remi had eaten the sock. One day Georgia and I were out walking and praying to Saint Lazarus at our usual spot in the park; Georgia was very tired that day, then a miracle happened. On the way home we got to our house and she started to dig feverishly at these two oval black stones. She wanted those stones so much; they were meant for her and she knew that. She was excited and smiling. Were they a sign from Saint Barbara and Saint Michael? I don't know but I picked up the stones and brought them into the house for her and put them by the statues of the Saints that protect us. Georgia seemed happy for the first time in weeks. A couple of days later the vet called us. Her tests showed a low normal for hypothyroid.

The vet put Georgia on medication for six weeks and then she was back to her normal self.

Things were good for a while in our household. I finally was doing well and could go back to work. Georgia was doing well, Remi was happy, Sydney was happy. Grandpa was happy. Everything was going good, but things happen.

My Angels, My Girls

13

THE EFFECTS ON US ALL

My father had an accident in January 2005. That accident, a simple slip and fall in a supermarket, kicked off a year of pure unadulterated hell, and change. My father's simple hip fracture caused him to have six surgeries and an incurable infection. For a better part of the year he was bedridden and for six months he would end up hospitalized. This in turn, changed all of our lives. Between my divorce and his illness we had to move from our beautiful house into a much smaller house. The most devastating part of the year was that May; Georgia was just about to turn nine and Sydney five. Remi had turned seven that January. We were all excited about moving into our new home that June, but we were all feeling rushed and anxiety ridden, as grandpa wasn't getting any better. Then on May 10, 2005; it happened. Remi the protector died. The night I brought her to the Emergency Animal Hospital, Georgia and Sydney were both extremely upset, but coming home that night without her was even worse. Sydney kept running around looking for her. Georgia just saw her collar and started whimpering. She knew. I think she sensed it when we left that REM REM wasn't coming back. Remi was like a daughter or a sister to Georgia, and to Sydney she was a mother or a sister. But she was the leader of the pack and now they were lost. Georgia was lost.

That was the first time my little Georgia wanted to be held like a baby since she was a baby. We both had lost our baby that day. Georgia took it very hard. I didn't realize how hard until she wouldn't let me put her down. My father had blamed himself, but it was no one's fault; it was just her time. Now she watches out for us from above. The day I brought her ashes home the girls went nuts. They could smell her essence. We howled a song for her and we still do now and then to honor her memory.

My Angels, My Girls

14

MOVING DAY

Moving day was unorganized and crazy. I had two trucks and one SUV stuffed full of our belongings and I could not fathom how I was going to fit all of our things into the smaller house that we were moving into. I had either sold or given a lot of our belongings to charity, but there still was so much. The girls, Georgia and Sydney, spent the night before moving day at their father's. And his girlfriend, she was not too happy about it nor he, but there was no way I could have handled two real estate closings, cleaning out one house and moving into another, plus worrying about my father who could not walk. I was lucky to have my aunt and cousin to take care of my dad that day. They took him to lunch and drove him to the new house, and the movers carried him in on a chair.

Surprisingly, everything managed to fit in the new house, although it appears a little cluttered with oversized furniture, but what can you do. It was finally time to go pick up Georgia and Sydney. I went to their father's house. The door was left unlocked and his girlfriend was out. I went inside and usually they give me trouble putting on their leashes (especially Sydney) but this time they gave me no trouble; they wanted out. I petted their stepbrother Aaron on the head. Their father had gotten another dog; a big sweet rottie-shepherd mix and we were out the door. I don't know what happened the night they stayed there. I know it wasn't their stepbrother because they love playing with him. When he comes to our house they play and are happy to see him, but when we go past their father's house to the dog park they cry. They are afraid that I am going to leave them there again.

We pulled up to our new house. They looked puzzled and a little apprehensive, were they being left again? I opened up the door, Sydney ran in of course, Georgia slowly walked in more cautiously, and then they saw my father and I could almost feel their sigh of relief. Sydney started exploring and Georgia too. But there were those horrible hardwood floors. Daddy's bedroom, and the dining room, which led to the deck to go outside, was hardwood floors; nice and shiny. And Sweetie Pie, she would have no part of those floors. She sat at the end of the living room looking in at Daddy, whimpering. It was so sad. She wanted to go in and see him. I lifted her up and carried her in so she could sit there with her grandpa.

After she explored his room for a while by walking all over his bed and giving it the once over, she decided she needed to go outside. I was a little leery about the girls' reaction to the fence out back. It was a privacy fence but it wasn't all that sturdy in places.

I walked my girls out to the backyard through the kitchen which was much easier for Georgia; she didn't have to walk on the hardwood floors this way. Thank God for small favors! My house was equipped with a breezeway through the kitchen that led out to the deck so my little princess could have an alternative entrance.

Georgia immediately went to the edge of the deck and let everyone know that she was there with a loud bark. "This is my home everyone. I'm Georgia, Let me introduce myself." She then sauntered off the deck and began her march around the yard, with a bark at each corner. Then from the next yard over a bark back; then a conversation commenced. Georgia found a friend; one that she couldn't see, but this became a daily ritual. I would eventually have to bring her in because Mouth Almighty would soon become overpowering with her vast vocal power. One would think a problem was developing and Sydney would soon chime in with her bark-howl, and we would have a free for all. I have been lucky once again. This has proven to be a dog friendly neighborhood.

The girls seemed to like their new home. I went out that evening to get some take-out from across the street and I brought it back. As we sat in my father's room eating, Georgia realized that if she wanted to get any table scraps she was going to have to conquer her fear of the dreaded wood floors. As she peeked in the bedroom, my father and I were eating our hot roast beef sandwiches and Sydney was right there along with us. Georgia stepped a little bit on the floor; one paw then the next, a little wobbly at first, but slowly she started making it into the bedroom until she was right by her grandpa, wagging her tail and barking her head off. She would not be denied; she wanted her share of the roast beef!

That night we all went to bed. I went upstairs to my bedroom and Georgia and Sydney scampered along behind me. My father went to sleep in his new bedroom and all was well. We were all content in our new house. Our little family.

The next morning I awoke to my father's horrific screaming. Blood and puss were all over the bed and floor. He had stood up and his incision in his leg had erupted with infection. I ran down the stairs.

Georgia jumped off my bed and down the stairs and started barking. Georgia hadn't jumped off a bed in years, so she must have been horrified by his scream. Sydney had beaten us both and was trying to lick the sore, trying to make it better. Right away, I grabbed the gauze and wound cleaner for my father and cleaned him up. My phone wasn't even connected yet, so I hunted for my cell phone and called his surgeon for what to do and then I cleaned up the mess on the floors and sheets. I had put Georgia and Sydney out in the yard while all this turmoil was going on. I didn't want them to be anymore traumatized or heaven forbid lick up any infection. The doctor called back and told me not to call an ambulance because I had to take him to a specific hospital, and to meet him. I called my girlfriend's husband who came over and helped me put my father into the car. I brought the girls in, and off to the hospital we went. My father got to see the house for one day, and then he spent the next six months in a hospital.

Georgia, Sydney and I would go through continuous stress over my father's illness, the loss of my job, the finalization of my divorce, the ups and downs of my on again off again relationship, who Georgia and Sydney began to think of as their new father, and the unpacking and decorating of our new house. All these things would affect us in different ways; our health, our personalities, and our spirituality.

We had all changed so deeply on three previous occasions; my stroke had taken a toll on all of us. The departure of my husband was one thing, but the loss of his friendship and his turning his back on the girls when he got his new girlfriend - that really hurt them. He never realized how much it hurt them. The look in their little eyes when he would come by; how he would play less and less with them to the point where he would practically push them away. There would be no more hide and seek with Secret Squirrel. They finally got to the point where they didn't even acknowledge that he even was there anymore. They were hurt. He would tell me I was ridiculous, that they couldn't feel. But they do, and they felt abandoned by him.

The final blow was REM REM's death. That changed all of us. She was the glue that held us together. The way she would howl, her running around checking on everyone, jumping on me when I would come in like "Dino" from the "Flintstones" cartoon. Her crazy antics, she always made you think everything was going to be all right.

No, we could not handle the loss of my father, too. Georgia, Sydney and I had to remain strong.

Georgia was the strongest of the three of us, or perhaps she was just trying to hide her feelings. She would wait at the door for me along with Sydney. She would try to keep Sydney calm. By this point she had become a total basket case. Georgia became the matriarch of our little pack and started taking care of both Sydney and me. My poor sweet Georgia was hiding all her own pain as she was taking care of us.

I was a nervous wreck, my father's condition was worsening, and he didn't even know how bad he actually was. I had lost my job. My husband who I had been separated from for three years decided to file for the final divorce papers at that moment. My boyfriend decided to do one of his famous disappearing acts because he couldn't handle the stress. His famous words are, "Things are "too complicated right now." Yes, it was a very bleak time. Sydney started having seizures, and with what happened to Remi, she was back and forth to the vet every other week. Poor little Georgia! She just took everything in her stride.

I started taking the girls to the hospital to see their grandpa every Sunday. I would have to take them together because I couldn't leave Sydney home alone for fear she would have a seizure. I would bring Sydney into the hospital first and let her see my father so she would settle down; then I would bring her out to the car and bring in Georgia so she could have her 10 minutes with my dad, then bring her out to the car. Then I would go in and say goodbye and bring them home. This kept our family together and helped my father stay out of a deep depression as well as the girls; they needed their grand pop. Of course, they had to deal with the little and bad resident Beagles just like Remi, but they were no match for Queen Mouth

Almighty and Sydney the Demon Child. They just took a one look at those two and I can only imagine what went through their little cute Beagle heads. Sydney - they probably thought she is a just plain nut and Georgia would give them this look and snippy bark "Don't mess with me! I'm here to see my grandpa and I have no time for your nonsense." There was none of the same following down the hall as with Remi, no territory breach - they just let them pass.

15

CHRISTMASTIME

Our first Christmas in our new house was a little lean because I still was not working. Melancholy because it was our first Christmas without REM REM, but it was full of miracles. Daddy had come home, Sydney's seizures had diminished, I had my maiden name back, and most importantly we were all together.

The doctors were unsure of my father; the infection was starting to rear its ugly head again. Other than that he was doing so well; walking with a cane, getting around on his own finally with minimal pain.

His doctor put him back on oral antibiotics but they did not see much hope considering this was the fourth round. They told us "We will see how he does through the holidays. If it gets worse, or no better, we will have to take the prosthesis out of the leg and he will be bedridden for the rest of his life." The doctor then looked at me and said, "Or he won't make it at all." My father was crushed, we all were. We had prayed for his homecoming for so long. We now needed a Christmas miracle.

We prayed. I would light candles to Saint Lazarus, and we prayed some more. We prayed to God, Jesus, the Blessed Mother, and the Saints. I would go to the cemetery with Georgia and sit by my mother. I now understood what she told me before she died; that I needed to take care of my father for her, and I asked her to intercede for my father to the Blessed Mother for us.

Christmas Eve, I took out REM REM's collar from the secretary where her ashes are kept, and we all thought about her, and Sydney, and Georgie cried and laid on her collar for a bit. We all howled a little in remembrance of her. I still had a candle burning to St. Lazarus in my father's bedroom. We were all gathered in the living room. Then there was a "Pop!" The candle in my father's room started burning wildly, the flame was high, flickering, quick; almost as if it was fighting itself, and the glass was becoming black. I was ready to snuff it out for fear that it would explode, but the flame finally calmed itself. Later on that evening, the candle went out on its own as it should when the novena is done.

My Angels, My Girls

The next morning, Christmas Day, my father called to me; I was petrified. Georgia, Syd and I ran down the stairs. He showed us his incision on his hip. The bubbling, infected lesion was gone. He then told me to look at the Saint Lazarus candle. I looked and within the burnt black glass that had encased the candle there was a shape of a dog. Now, for those of you who don't know anything about Saint Lazarus he is usually shown walking with two dogs. Now it could be a coincidence that the candle started burning wildly after I took Rem Rem's collar out and Sydney and Georgia started crying and howling, and maybe their prayers reached Remi to intercede to Saint Lazarus and God for Daddy and us, but whatever happened that Christmas Eve, by Christmas morning we had our miracle. The doctor even agreed that some sort of miracle had taken place when we went to see him that following week. I believe his exact words were "Did you take a trip to Lourdes?" I just looked at him and said "Yeah, something like that!" My father's continued healing I believe has been a combination of finally finding the right medical expertise, faith, grace, love and a large part of his continued healing is those two little crazy girls. Georgia and Sydney, his grand dogs. He loves and lives for them.

Yes, it was a wonderful first Christmas in our new home. Georgia and Sydney got everything they wanted and they had their grandpoppy home and for Georgia that was all that mattered. She just would sit there and watch him smiling from ear to ear. Sydney would play with her new toys and be obliviously happy.

We had made it through. We were finally accepting REM REM's death, but realizing that she was still around, and Daddy was finally on his way to a complete recovery. I could sit back and breathe. It was then that I noticed Georgia's hair still hadn't really grown back in from the summer, she wasn't bald or anything, but her hair wasn't growing back. Some of it was, but it was patchy.

16

IS IT OR ISN'T IT?

Georgia was nine and a half the summer before when we first moved in to the new house. Her weight was over but she has always been a little overweight. Her hair had just been shaved that May so I really didn't notice that it was growing back at such a slow pace. Now I was noticing everything. Georgia was beginning to wheeze and she would lie around in my bedroom; she just didn't want to be bothered. She was gaining weight again and her hair - she looked like a burn victim it was so patchy. I took her to the vet and once again, the C word. CUSHINGS. "She has all the signs but the testing is expensive. Do you want us to test her for it?" "Do I want her tested for it? What do you think?" "Test Her!" I hate to be so curt with a vet because I know some people can't afford to have their animals tested, but then, I'm me. I remember being in a vet's office one day and wanting to pay for this puppy's rabies shot because this young couple couldn't afford both shots, but they were gone when I came out. Luckily the next time I was there they were back getting him the rest of his shots. It's a shame employers don't offer pet insurance, but some employers don't even offer health insurance, so I guess I'm asking too much. We have to deal with the costs the same as with human health care; that can be outrageous to say the least.

Purchasing pet insurance on your own is expensive in its own right, and like health insurance for human beings, it has the same exclusions for pre-existing conditions. Unless you pay for a ryder. Don't pay for preventive care or just pay for preventive care, but don't pay for anything else. Insurance companies! I don't want to get on my soapbox, but whether it's for humans or pets, if you ask me, in my opinion, well we won't go into that it's like politics and religion you really don't want to get in a discussion about it because everyone has their opinion and unfortunately you have to play the cards your dealt when it comes to insurance. So, for pet insurance; I guess it may be worth it if your vet accepts it, especially if you can get one that pays for their annual inoculations because that can run into some pretty hefty bills, especially if you have more than one four-legged child. It would definitely be worth it. God forbid if your child ends up with a problem such as cancer or heart problem or needs some type of surgery. Unfortunately, most that I have looked into say they should be insured as a pup. I will have to investigate that option further. Also what I have found with pet insurance is you have to pay for the procedures first and then you submit the claim and they reimburse you for 60 or 80 percent. It's great to have the money back in your pocket but what happens if you don't have the money to pay for the procedure in the first place and your paying a monthly insurance premium? You are pardon the expression, "screwed". Like I said, I need to investigate that topic further. It is only my opinion so don't get me on the topic of insurance (we won't get back to my babies). In REM REM's case it would not have mattered if I had insurance because it happened so fast and the hospital I took her to did not have a ventilator to do the surgery she needed. And she would not have survived the drive to the hospital that had a ventilator. But if she did, I was told that surgery would have cost in the neighborhood of five to six thousand dollars and I would still be paying that off now. I guess pet insurance might be worth looking into. Don't even get me started on heartworm and flea & tick preventative, but they are worth it every bit of the expense. Even when they hate you for putting that flea & tick preventative on and they're running away while you are trying to put it on them. Ever try to put that little tube on the four spots of their back and they don't want it there? It's a challenge. I'm sure you are with me on this, but we do it anyway because we love them. Then watch them go roll in the dirt trying to get it off because they hate it. At least, in my case, they like their heartworm pills. They think it is a treat.

Well, enough of my rant. Back to Georgia's testing; she had her blood work for the dreaded CUSHINGS and for her Thyroid again. Poor little girl; they had to stick her twice because they missed the vein. Georgia I'll reiterate again is not good with vets. She is better if they are female, but she is still petrified of them, and because of that she needs to be muzzled. My little sweetie pie was frantic this day. She was muzzled, they missed sticking her, and had to stick her a second time. I could see the look of fear in her eyes and the little tears streaming down her little face. I kept petting her, trying to keep her calm, but she was almost hyperventilating I was almost crying myself. Finally, they were done, and they took the muzzle off. I just held her and as heavy as she was (Georgia weighs 39 pounds) I carried her out of the vets office that day, like I did when she was a pup. I put her in the car and when we got home I carried her into the house like a baby. I set her down in the house on her favorite rug. A little while later my little sweetie pie made her way back upstairs to my room and laid on her favorite doggy bed. She would move from there to a little spot in my room, where on my dresser a statue of Saint Lazarus and Saint Michael stood with her stones that she found a couple of years before. She would lay there for a bit then go back to her bed.

I would come up to bed later on and put her in bed with me. Sydney would follow, and Georgia always had to be on the end near her statues watching the candles. She was mesmerized by the flickering of the flames. I used to look at her, even now I still do, and I swear I think she actually prays. I prayed waiting for those tests to come back; I lit candles. Georgia and I sat there praying to Saint Lazarus and Saint Francis once again, we went to the cemetery to see my mother's grave and once again we looked to Remi and cried. My father was particularly worried. Georgia was his baby, and all she wanted to do was hide in my room by her statues.

The vet finally called me with the test results. She had hypothyroid bordering on Cushings, but it was not Cushings. My prayers once again had been answered. I wasn't happy that she had a thyroid problem, but at least it wasn't Cushings. Our vet put her on medication and at first the dosage was too strong, which actually made her sicker, but once she was put on the correct amount My Old Girl started showing improvement right away. Georgia stopped hiding by her statues, but she didn't stop praying to her candles at night. She would still sleep on that side of the bed and look like she was praying or talking to her statues. Her energy level increased, and she started to play with Sydney a little bit, and most impressive, her hair started to grow back. Georgia's hair growing back not only made me happy because it showed physical signs that she was starting to get well, but it made Sweetie Pie happy as well. Georgia, always being the vain one hated the fact that her hair was not growing in right. Now that her hair was starting to grow back, she got that prance back in her step and in her eyes. She was ready for the groomer. I still wanted to wait until it got longer and all the bald spots were covered. I wanted to make sure that her skin would not be irritated by any shampoos. I just brushed her at home and she loved it. Each day her condition improved, her smile improved, and as my father's condition improved her smile grew larger. Everything was finally working out for our little pack.

My Angels, My Girls

17

A NEW TRANSITION

My father's condition was finally improving and with Georgia on the mend I was able to go back to work. I was lucky to be offered two positions at the same time; one in my field and one in a completely different direction in a very young, dynamic office which I jokingly referred to my friends as Model, Inc., because it seemed as though you had to be a model to work there. Everyone was so young, fresh, gorgeous and fit. Anyway, I chose the job at Model, Inc., which really isn't the name, or what they did. Although it was less money, it was closer and was something completely different. I was one of the lucky ones who actually like the people they work with and love her bosses. Maybe my next book will be about the crazy antics that go on behind the scenes of my office. It might actually make a funny reality TV show. They knew all about the crazy antics of my girls and they don't mind listening to my stories about them, so I think I picked the right job. One of them even had the distinct pleasure of meeting them, and Sydney gave him her special "Hello" that she gives all new people that come into our house. He was extremely surprised, but that story will come a little later on, in the book of Sydney.

I am off my mark again, how about that! I need to get back to how Georgia and Sydney, especially Georgia, handled the transition of me going back to work after seven months. Can you say "NOT HAPPY?"

Georgia would not speak to me when I went back to work. I would come home at night and she would go sit next to my father or by the sliding doors in the dining room and stick her nose up in the air. Sydney on the other hand would show her dissatisfaction by peeing in the hallway outside my bedroom and pulling the trash out of my bathroom and scattering it from one end of my bedroom to the other. I nipped that in the bud by shutting the door to the bedroom upstairs. Yes, it took them quite awhile to get used to the fact that I was back to work. I think they were afraid more than angry that someone was leaving them again. After all they are like little children and they have strong feelings of abandonment, too. Once they realized that I was coming home every night, like children they started to get acclimated to the situation. But if they had their way I would never leave the house without them. Although Sydney no longer destroys things, I still get cold shoulders from the both of them if I go anywhere other than work. God forbid if my father goes anywhere with me and we leave them home by themselves. The TV has to be on and they don't want Animal Planet on like most dogs; they want Discovery Kids and the light has to be left on in case it gets dark out. And we better be darn sure we bring them a treat home or there will be hell to pay. Yes, they are spoiled rotten, but they deserve it.

Transitions kept happening, Georgia kept going with the flow, and her grandpa was improving. Her father was coming around less and less; he had another new girlfriend who he was making a new home with and when he would come over he would rarely play with her anymore; just a pat on the head, and tell me how bad she looked, all patchy with her hair or how fat she was. There was no more hide and seek for little Secret Squirrel; you could see in her eyes that she was hurt. Eventually, she would stop running out to see him and just sit by my father on the floor by the couch, or just stay in the dining room by the sliding glass door, looking out at the yard. She just didn't care anymore. He didn't exist to her. She had her grandpa and her mommy; that is all she needed. I know I have brought this up earlier in the story - the distancing of her father - but it is important that people realize how animals feel. Divorces hurt everyone, we talk about the toll it takes on the kids, but it takes a toll on the pets too. I know a couple who divorced. She was bitter, and never let him see his dog. Eventually the dog died and she didn't even let him know that his dog died. That was wrong. He was horribly upset when he found out. He loved that dog. Animals are not possessions. They are special gifts with souls that are meant to accompany us through life, and the sooner we realize the better.

Sydney felt it too. He slowly distanced himself from her. Each time he would come over, playing with her less and less each time. Each visit was shorter and shorter. Sydney finally would just sit there on the couch and look at him, but he had left the house. When Syd was little she liked to play with him and her stepbrother Aaron, who I think she actually misses more. Neither one of them has seen their father since before Christmas. They had gifts for their stepbrother and him, but he didn't want to visit them.

It is funny, people think that animals don't remember holidays or people that meant something to them, or did something to them, or loved them for a little while, but they do. Animals remember love, trauma, hate, and abandonment. Why do you think if you raise your hand to a dog and the dog had been hit before it cowers or attacks? That dog remembers. It is the same if that dog remembers love or abandonment by a person. It is going to remember. The animal is going to have some feeling of joy, love, pain, or sadness. My girls know their father left; and they know that he left again when he stopped visiting them, which hurt them more. They felt the pain of loss when REM REM died. They were petrified of losing my father and felt his pain when he was sick. Sydney would try to lick his sores, and they felt my pain when I was sick. REM REM was able to sense when a seizure was coming on and I would wake up with her on top of me protecting me making sure that I would not fall out of bed. They sensed the emotional trauma I went through with my stroke, the fear of not being able to walk again. They showed their support by laying their heads on my lap or howling when I cried. They felt my father's illness, my fear and their own fear of losing him. My point in all of this is that they may be animals to some of you, but realize first and foremost they are living breathing souls, and they feel love and pain like any human being. I cannot stress this enough.

Life continued, and with it brought the return of my boyfriend. Sydney was happy she got her playmate back. She was young when her father left and my boyfriend was more of a father to her than her father. Georgia, not so much; it meant sharing her mother again. Sharing her bed and worrying when the other shoe was going to drop and she didn't like seeing her mom sad; neither did Sydney for that matter. Unfortunately, Georgia being an old soul of sorts is much more wary of people; always the better watchdog than Sydney, and a better judge of character than Sydney and perhaps her Mommy. She would watch my boyfriend come back and forth and be there for a while and see Sydney and me both happy; then he would leave again. I would be hurt, Sydney would be crushed. I think that is why she never allowed herself to get close to him; or perhaps Georgia's main concern was her bed, she had gotten mighty comfortable in that big king size bed with her mommy to the point where she would give Sydney the ol' growlly growl if Sydney invaded her space.

Yes, Georgia did not like anyone in her bed. Even if one of my girlfriends would stay over she just liked it to be me and her and she would allow Sydney. But Sydney had to fight for her place on the bed and that had gone on while Remi was alive. Remi would not allow Sydney on the bed. It was a regular war every night. I'll go more into that when I tell Sydney's story but now we are talking about Georgie and her trials and tribulations. Her wars with Sydney over the bed are a little more subdued as long as they keep to their neutral corners. I do not wish to make it sound as if they don't get along because they do love each other; that is evident. But they are definitely sisters, and the sibling rivalry runs deep.

Sydney loves to torment Georgia. Sydney is the baby and loves to play. Georgia is old, the matriarch and doesn't. Well, just the other night, Georgia, who never has accidents in the house, decided she had enough of Sydney's shenanigans. Sydney has this spot that she likes to lay between my bedroom and hallway if she is not sleeping in the bed. Well, Georgia decided to take a major pee in that spot. Then she walked away and had this look on her face, "Well there, gotcha" and she just looked like she was laughing this sneaky little laugh. "Come on Syd, come up the stairs and lay down. I dare ya." Of course, I cleaned up the mess, and the whole time she just sat there with this smile on her face. She reminded me of this dog I used to see on a cartoon when I was a child. I wish I could remember the name that would sit there laughing this funny but diabolical HEHEHEHE!!! Sydney came up the stairs and looked at her, smelled her spot, huffed and went downstairs for the night. This morning while Georgia was trying to drink some water, Sydney walked over, stood over top of her and started drinking right over her. Sydney usually waits until Georgia is done, out of respect. The war is on. Mind you, they would never hurt each other, and each would come to the other's aid; but after last night Georgia crossed the line and now they will be tormenting each other and fighting until they either get tired of it or I yell at them for it, because I am sick of it.

Georgia, my Old Girl, Sweetie Pie, Secret Squirrel, The Queen, Mouth Almighty. My God, that nick name fits her best. She has been with me now 11 years, she has seen so much, taken in so much, been through so much, as she sits there with that little smile, those black coal eyes and pink nose. I still see the little snowball I brought home all those years ago, the fact that she still hasn't grown back all her hair or is still heavy because of her thyroid doesn't bother me. I cry seeing my little girl waddle around in pain when there is bad weather because she now has a touch of arthritis.

No matter what, she still is my little Sweetie Pie. Even when she gets constipated and gets poop stuck in her little butt and tries to hide it from me. "Georgia, let me see your butt," I'll say. She will get this look of determination on her face and sit there and not let me near her butt, she will even run from me. Seriously, she will do everything she can so I won't get near her butt. Finally, I will win and put her in the sink and clean her all out. At first she will be stiff and growling or crying by the end she is smiling from ear to ear. Yeah, she's happy she's got that nasty stuff out of her butt. She's a little lady she doesn't like to be stinky and uncomfortable.

Georgia finally got to go back to the groomer this past Christmas when her hair had grown in enough that I was satisfied she wouldn't be hurt or irritated. She was so happy. We walked into the shop. It was a new place, but it was almost as if she knew where she was. She went straight away with the groomer and when I picked her up she thought she was the Bell of the Ball. Later that day, she went to have her picture taken with Santa. We hadn't done that in quite a few years. I think that made her year. She got so much attention from the patrons at the store, and Santa and the workers that she thought she was a celebrity. She went down each of the aisles sniffing out what she wanted for Christmas, sending her Christmas wishes to Santa. Christmas 2006 was definitely the best one in a long time. If only Remi could have been there that would have made it perfect.

Now I play hide and seek with my Secret Squirrel, her favorite thing is to surprise me in the morning by sneaking from under the blankets and giving me a big kiss or just laying there looking at me in the morning, front paws crossed right up in my face and as soon as my eyes open planting one on me. Once I get up out of the bed I pick her up, give her a big hug, rub her belly and put her down on the floor. Then we walk downstairs together. She can't get down from the bed alone, and she always waits for me to walk down the stairs for fear of Syd lurking at the bottom to torment her. At night, I hear the jingle of her coming up the hallway, and she lies at the foot of the bed waiting for me to pick her up and I do, like a baby. Then I give her a little airplane ride and swing. I put her on the bed and she walks around the bed fluffing the pillows, finding her spot which is always by her statues - unless she is in a cuddly mood - then she gets under the blankets and makes her way over to me and pops her head out and goes to sleep in my arms.

My sweetie pie, she is in her golden years now. She'll be 11 this May. My father teases her all the time, "Georgia, Old Girl you are almost as old as me, next year you will be older than me." Georgia just sits there and wags her tail smiling away. They are a pair; her and my father. My first little girl, my first Angel, my oldest, dearest, grouchiest and loudest, and she will always be by my side laughing and protecting our family, patrolling the perimeter of the property line, making sure that nothing gets in HER yard. My little watchdog! The complete opposite of my third little Angel, my baby, my demon child, my Syd Vicious, my little instigator, my Sydney, my little Sydney Sue.

18

SYDNEY

Sydney was born on May 25, 2000 and came into our lives approximately 12 weeks later. Sydney basically was brought into our home when my ex-husband and I were trying to save our marriage. We had tried for years to have children to no avail the fertility treatments were weakening my heart; I had a mild heart attack that past March. Little did I know what was to come, how bad my heart was, and that attack was a precursor to a stroke two years later. My doctor had suggested adoption but no more fertility treatments. My husband wasn't too thrilled about that, which added to our marital problems. Sydney appeared to be the answer. Unfortunately she wasn't the solution for our situation, but she has become the most important part of my life and perhaps the most feeling and human of all my little Angels. One thing is for sure; she is truly my little baby, would never hurt a fly or any other living being, and a watchdog she is not.

The day we saw Sydney at the puppy store (the same shop where we had previously gotten Georgia and REM REM) it was an accident. We had planned on adopting this little pup from a shelter, but the puppy was adopted out from under us because we didn't have our vet information on us that day. I'm sure that he went to a good home and I'm sure that fate had a hand in us getting Sydney. We had been at the Cemetery earlier that day visiting my mother's grave and my husband needed to stop by Home Depot, which was right next store to the puppy store. I was depressed and could not resist going in to play with the pups. I walked in, and in the "On Sale" crate was this skinny, little, runt with a little half shuteye, which gave the appearance that she was winking. She was so cute with these big floppy paws, a little diamond shaped mask and deep blue eyes. She looked so sad and tiny for a husky.

I asked the shopkeeper, "Why is she on sale?" She replied, "She's been here six weeks already. No one has taken to her. I think because of her eye, and she is so tiny for a husky." I asked, "How old is she, and what is wrong with her eye?" "She is about 12 weeks old and her eye is a lazy eye. She might grow out of it as she gets older, or it might get worse and require surgery, or she might have problems seeing with that eye." "People also are concerned with her size for a husky. She is so small," she responded. "They also think she looks evil." She just laid there. This pitiful little thing in a little ball, occasionally looking around with this little puss on her face. No smile, not trying to get anyone's attention, all alone in this "On Sale" crate. She looked like she was put in a "Time Out." I felt so sorry for her. She looked like the way I was feeling inside; abandoned and lost.

My husband had finally entered the store at this point. I said to him, "I want her." He said, "Are you kidding? Another Husky?" "I thought you couldn't deal with Huskies. Come on, you know how hard they are to train." "We haven't even housebroken Remi yet. And look at her. What is wrong with her eye?" "I wanted a male dog, a bigger dog. She is so small. Are you sure she is even a Husky?" At that point, I picked her up and pushed her to him, "Look at her, look at that mask and those eyes." "You tell me she isn't a husky!" She opened her eyes really wide almost like she was trying, and he held her. "Okay," "We'll get her but she is getting crate trained and house broken, she is not going to be another Remi, and I am naming her." Well, we decided that second to name her Sydney, before we even left the shop. The Olympics were going on in Sydney, Australia at that time. Besides she took to the name right away and the name for some reason just fit her.

We left the store like the two times before with Georgia and Remi. I had Sydney on my lap wrapped in my seatbelt with me. Only something was different with this little one. She kept crawling up and trying to rest her head on my heart. She purred like Georgia and kissed me like Remi but this one, she had to rest her head on my heart and kept looking up at me to kiss me right on the mouth. I thought "how sweet" and her little half closed eye kept winking at me. I thought to myself, "How anyone could think this precious little thing looked evil?" I thought her diamond markings on her face, her deep blue eyes, and black and white coat made her beautiful. Her oversized pointy ears, big paws, and lets not forget her tongue that was too big for her mouth, just made her stupendously adorable and her big black nose and mouth. She was just absolutely gorgeous. I had completely fallen in love with my new baby. I didn't know what a devil in disguise she would be, not a bad devil mind you, but she would certainly turn our house upside down from the moment we walked in the door.

When we walked into the house, REM REM and Georgia came running out only to be taken aback by the little surprise we brought home with us. Needless to say they were not pleased, and my father he just threw up his arms. "Another one, he shouted, are you crazy?" Shaking his head in disbelief as he sat down on the couch with Remi and Georgia who just looked at little Syd with her half closed eye, and us with an over powering look of disdain. Sydney just cowered behind my leg, sniffing around the kitchen, with this little whimper all the while not straying too far from the safety of my legs. She was trembling scared of REM REM & Georgie and the fact that they didn't immediately welcome her. I was afraid that this living situation wasn't going to work out. My dad kept reinforcing that idea; "Remi and Georgia aren't happy with this," he would say. "You shouldn't have gotten another one, what's wrong with her?" My poor little baby! Everyone picked on her. Georgia and Remi just shunned her that day. They would sniff her and walk away. Georgia would bark at her and REM REM would talk to her in a mocking tone. I wish I understood dog but I knew it wasn't nice because Sydney would just go curl up in a corner. Georgia and Remi would look at me and with a huff go lay by their grandpa. It was not the happy homecoming I had hoped for Sydney.

I had a big food trough in the kitchen for the girls to share their dry dog food. Remi and Georgia used to eat out of it simultaneously, or Remi would patiently wait for Georgia and vice-versa. The water bowls were next to it with fresh water. Sydney spied the food and darted for it, she started eating like she never saw food before; Remi decided to walk over to see what she was doing. After all it was her food and she started to stare Syd down and nudge her a bit. The next thing I see and hear is Sydney growling and showing her teeth. Well, that does not go on in my house; I think Remi was even a bit surprised by it even though she stood her ground and just stared back at her. No growling, no teeth gnashing; just an intimidating stare. Remi, being the size she was, if she wanted to, could have snapped Sydney in two and she knew it. In Remi's mind, she was probably thinking "Who does this little scrawny brat think she is?" Sydney continued eating and growling. Georgia came running over; she had had enough and started barking. I had enough. I pulled her away from the dish and gave her a little smack on the nose and told her in a stern voice "NO." At that point she cocked her head to the side and then she looked to the floor and let out a small whimper. I think she actually understood, she moved out of the way and let her sisters in and watched them eat together out of the food bowl and drink together out of the water bowl. She watched as Remi waited for Georgia to finish patiently by the water how they didn't shove at each other and how they ate together. The entire time she watched, her head would cock from one side then to the other as she was trying to decipher this new way of living; not trying to fight for food, and being able to share. There was plenty. She was going to get all she wanted and she didn't have to be aggressive to get it.

Remi was eating now. Sydney walked a couple of feet very cautiously towards her. She was still hungry, but after what happened she didn't know what to do. Sydney kept looking back at me tilting her head, looking at REM REM, the food, taking a couple more steps. I could see Remi looking at her, out of the corner of her eye, deciding what she was going to do; Georgia already had her fill and was back by her Grandpa and Daddy relaxing. Quick as a whip, Remi spun around and said, "Ru Ru RRRR Ru Ru," right in Sydney's face. I swear Sydney's ears went straight

166

backward and her eyes opened in sheer terror. Trembling, she ran behind my legs. Remi went back to eating looking back at Sydney with this half smirk on her face. I slowly brought Sydney over to the food trough. Remi was side-eyeing us the whole time. I said, "Come on Remi this is your new little sister, now you show how nice you are and be good and share." "Sydney this is your big sister Remi you be good too and share." Sydney tilted her head and looked at me, then at REM REM. Remi looked up from the food bowl, looked at me, then at Syd who stood there with her head and tail lowered submissively. Then Remi moved over and made space for Sydney to eat along side of her. As they continued to eat, Sydney would kiss Remi on the ear. It started looking like she was actually cleaning Remi's ears by the end of the meal. Whether she liked it or not Remi had an adopted pup because I believe that Sydney thought of Remi not as a sister but more as a Mommy. Georgia has slowly made her way back into the kitchen by this time and decided, "Okay the little runt isn't so bad," and went up to Sydney and started sniffing her again and wagging her tail. Sydney started cleaning her ears too, but she learned quickly that the Old Matriarch had to be in the mood for an ear cleaning or she would get the old growlly growl. We made it through dinner without anyone ripping each other apart. My husband was upstairs putting together the crate for little Syd Vicious to sleep in so we could properly crate train her. She still had only uttered a whimper but at least she was starting to warm up to Georgia and Remi and they were warming up to her. Even my dad was starting to warm up to her. "Definitely the runt of the litter. Poor little thing, you can tell by the way she was with the food." "She better change her ways with that or REM REM will put her in her place." "Georgia won't put up with her either," he would say.

Later on that night, we all went up to bed. We put little Syd in the crate under the window with a tee shirt and set it up like we set it up for Georgia and REM REM. Georgia went to bed next to me on the floor, and Remi went to bed on the floor at the bottom of the bed in front of the doorway; their normal spots. My husband and I retired. We shut out the lights and were not in bed 15 minutes before Sydney started crying. It started with a small whimper and escalated into an ear-piercing wail. There was nothing that we could do to. We turned on the lights; Sydney was screaming. You could see the tears streaming down her face as she clawed at the crate. Then Remi started howling, and of course Georgia had to start barking too. We gave up, opened the crate and let Sydney out. We turned on the TV and we all got in bed, my husband, me, and all three girls. I was holding Sydney in my arms. She was finally calming down, but then the green-eyed jealousy monster hit Remi and she nipped Sydney right on the ear. Sydney let out a wail that could have awakened the dead. I smacked Remi on the snout. I hated ever smacking my girls at all. Everything happened so fast, Sydney was screaming, burying her head in my chest, Georgia was barking and REM REM ran away howling. She was hurt. I smacked my poor REM REM. Even though she had nipped Sydney on the ear, I didn't have to smack her on the nose. She wasn't physically hurt, her pride was hurt and I realized at that moment she felt that she was being replaced. She was no longer the baby, and she had to grow up. I guess Remi felt like I abandoned her like Georgia did when we had brought Remi home.

I put Sydney in the bed and set off downstairs to find Remi, she was laying on her favorite couch in the living room sulking. I went over to her and I hugged her and I told her sweetly in her ear, "REM REM she's your little sister. You need to watch out for her. No one is ever going to replace you or Georgia." "You are Mommy's big wolf, Mommy's big girl, you need to help little Sydney, make her feel welcome." "She already looks to you." Remi just lay there pouting away, nostrils flaring. "I'm sorry I smacked you Remi, I didn't mean to, you scared me when you bit her, she is so little." With that, she looked up at me, then she went back to her pout, then she looked up again, stretched and jumped off the couch and ran up the stairs. I went up after her and there they were my husband, Georgia,

Sydney and now Remi all in the bed; Remi was lying next to Sydney and kissing her ear. I got into bed and we all shared the bed that night. Sydney fell asleep next to my heart listening to it beat, Georgia in the middle of the bed and Remi at the bottom. My husband was hanging on for dear life, and that was the end of Sydney's first night and the beginning of her life with us.

Sydney spent her first week or two sleeping in bed with me like that. She was quite the baby. Then it was time for her to go to the dreaded vet. Since we got her so late she had already had her shots, and her first trip to the vet was to get fixed. She still was so quiet and timid; when I took her to the vet's office she just looked back and went off with the technician. I think she thought I was leaving her there. She just looked back and let out a little cry, put her tail and head down and walked down the hall, occasionally looking back at me with this pitiful stare. She would look back like she was walking her last mile. I guess she thought she was. God! The girl could get an Oscar for giving guilt trips. Of course, my poor little Sydney had to be my only child who would get deathly ill from the anesthesia. Georgia had a problem waking up from it, which was scary, and little sick Remi pulled out of it like a champ. Sydney was up all night sick, and pardon the expression, sick as a dog. We were up and down with her. If the poor thing wasn't puking she needed water, and we had to be careful she didn't strain the stitches. Oh those horrible stitches, she was the only one who had to wear the dreaded e-collar to keep her away from her stitches. What a mess! I think she learned how to be double jointed from that incident. She was going to get her mouth on those stitches if it killed her, e-collar

or no e-collar.

19

SYDNEY'S FIRST

CHRISTMAS

It was nearing Christmas and I wanted badly to take my girls to see Santa. It would be Sydney's first time. My husband and I were not getting along and he really didn't want to be bothered with taking all three of them at the same time to see Santa. I suggested going separately but of course that was a chore too. I guess I can't blame him completely. We both were pretty much involved in our separate lives by that point and our family life was suffering. We were trying to make it a good Christmas for everyone but the child/doggy care was beginning to fall more and more on my father, as my husband and I grew further and further apart and more and more into our careers. Unfortunately because of this, Sydney would not get to meet Santa until she was much older, and poor Remi, bless her soul, never got to see him again.

Sydney was slowly growing into herself, she was seven months old that first Christmas and the devil in her was starting to show. Remi had decided months ago that Sydney was no longer allowed to sleep in bed with Mommy every night. That had to be shared and she was showing her leadership qualities over the household. Georgia, always the Old Girl and Matriarch, would not take any flack from either of them. Remi had tired of Sydney being the little baby and Sydney in turn had tired of Remi being the boss of her.

I had bought the girls little jingle bell collars to wear for the holidays. I always liked dressing the girls up at Christmas but nothing more than bandanas or collars would fly. Well, Christmas was interesting enough now with three; each with their little collars, scampering around, greeting the Christmas Eve guests eating, drinking, and finally it was time to open presents and take pictures. The girls were very excited about this. Sydney was especially excited but she didn't know how things worked and of course REM REM was going to show her. The next thing I'm hearing is a big scuffle in the kitchen and they both come walking in with Christmas wrapping paper and bows stuck to them. Remi looks disgusted and takes a seat on her favorite couch and shoots Sydney this look and curls up in a little ball. I look at Sydney, her mouth is full of something, "Sydney that better not be chocolate!" I said, and with that she spits out the jingle bells from Remi's collar and starts barking at REM REM, and stamping her two front paws. Lovely; another one that stamps her paws. And a husky that barks but does not talk; this is different. After she was done she jumped on the other end of the couch, Remi's favorite couch, mind you, with a huff, and just looked at REM REM. Remi glared back. They both curled up in little balls and stared at each other from the opposite ends of that couch. Yes, Remi met her match on that Christmas Eve. Sydney showed there would be no more backing down from anyone not even REM REM, and the couch became shared along with everyone and everything else. My husband, father and I just sat there and laughed at the whole situation, especially when she walked in and just spit out those bells. Georgia got this look of fear in her eyes thinking that she was now outnumbered, but Syd and Rem always respected and protected Georgia as well as each other. But the tormenting and teasing would now and always be a way of life.

The next year would prove to be an interesting one as Sydney's devilish ways infiltrated the house more and more. She was still petite but her eye was appearing to get better. It was opening bigger and bigger. She didn't look like she was winking anymore. Her diamond mask was now looking more like a spade and she was now growing into her paws, but her tongue was still not growing into her head as she approached her first birthday. She would run around the yard, her tongue would be flapping in the breeze, but her demeanor was changing. She was a devil and a prankster, but she was becoming the most good-natured and affectionate little girl you ever saw. The little puppy that was so stand-offish and never smiled was now jumping on everyone that came into the house; wanting everyone's attention kissing everyone. Unfortunately she had this one annoying habit of sniffing everyone's crotches and backsides. She definitely was no longer shy. Luckily she would only sniff those who she did not know or those she knew very well as if it was her way of saying hello. To this day I still try to break her of this habit. I'll finally think she's done with it, then, out of the blue she will do it again. Sydney was growing up. She was happy; she actually smiles and you can see it when she smiles. Her lip actually wrinkles up to a smirk and you can see her front fang on one side. She looks like a little vampire when she smiles. She and Remi would just run and run all over the yard and chase each other until they would get so tired they would fall down and lay in the sun.

Georgia would bark at them as they ran circles around her, then they would all line up. My three little bathing beauties out in the yard! They were so happy.

Sydney still had severe crate and abandonment issues, even if her sisters were with her. I took the three of them to the groomer one day and the groomer called me at noon and asked me to come pick Sydney and Remi up because they were making too much noise. Georgia was fine, but Sydney and Remi were crying and barking too much. Every time Sydney was put in the crate she would claw and moan until they put her in the crate with Remi, but together they would make twice as much noise. Remi was never like this before Syd; as long as she could see Georgia she was fine. I never was called to the groomer because she made too much noise and was crying too much. Baby Syd, she was a little instigator.

My Angels, My Girls

20

THE ADVENTURES OF

SYD & REM

As Remi grew up she would occasionally get out and we would have to go after her. I can still see her as a pup climbing that chain link fence in our first home; link by link, toe by toe, up and over, and down the back street, but the safe thing about my little Remi - she knew she wasn't supposed to do that and she always had a fear of getting in trouble with her father. Although she wanted to roam she was content to do it on the end of a leash. She liked running with me holding on to her but then we would tire to a nice brisk walk, then to a slow, lazy glide the rest of the way home. Georgia hadn't had an urge to run and roam in pardon the expression "a dog's age." She was content with her walks on the leash. As a matter of fact she looked forward to a leisurely stroll so she could take in the sights. Besides, if she did decide to run she was getting to that age that she would be pretty easy to catch. Sydney, my demon child, was coming into her own and she was teaching her sisters, especially REM REM, bad habits.

It was hurricane season and my husband and I were at work. My father had gone outside to get the paper. When he came back in he shut and locked the front door, but he did not shut the door hard enough. A strong wind came by and blew the front door wide open. My father who was upstairs at the time did not realize this, and Sydney saw it as the opportunity she had been waiting for to explore, and she took Remi with her. Georgia sat quietly on the front porch but did not move from there. She just waited for her sisters to return. I do not know how long they were gone. My father does not know because he was upstairs. But he says to this day he was not upstairs that long when he got the phone call from one of our distant neighbors that lived about a mile away. "Hi, do you own two Huskies? I found them playing in my garage." My dad actually told the lady at first that it couldn't be our girls because they were downstairs, until she said their names. She had told him that her house had been on fire and she was cleaning it out and had the garage doors open and she found them in there. It had started raining again and they went in there for shelter; thank God for the rain and dog tags. Who knows where they would have ended up? The nice neighbor lady kept them there until my father drove over and picked them up. Sydney the little demon, Remi never would have gone that far on her own! My father told my husband and me the story of their little excursion when we returned home from work that evening. Needless to say we were not pleased. I was always afraid that they would get lost, hit by a car or worse. Sydney and Remi both just sat there mighty happy with their selves; they had been out exploring the world.

Sydney hated being on a leash. I had bought a double lead to walk Syd and Rem on so Georgia could be walked separately in peace. The turmoil that would ensue just trying to get Sydney attached to the leash was catastrophic. Her screaming and jumping around would even give Remi (a.k.a. Monk Monk) a run for her money. Finally, with everyone hooked up to their leads, I would open up the front door and an immediate race would begin. Sydney would tangle herself and Remi up so badly by two houses down that we would have to stop. Syd and Rem rolled all over each other and Remi yelled at Sydney and Sydney screamed back. Georgia would just mosey along with my dad, look at both of them, smirk, "losers" and walk right on past them laughing, enjoying her stroll. I would finally get them untangled; we would start walking, and darn if Sydney wouldn't do it again. The problem with Sydney I think was she was left for so long at the store and from where ever she was bred that now she always wanted to be first. No matter what it was, whether it was the first to eat, the first out the door or in the door, first on the leash off the leash Sydney had to be first. And Remi was having none of it because up until the arrival of Sydney, she was the leader of the pack and she was going to make sure little Syd Vicious understood this at all costs. So every walk would continue to be an adventure with each of them fighting to maintain the position of lead.

21

MY STROKE

The days following my stroke were particularly hard on my girls and me. My stint in the rehabilitation center and the departure of my husband had filled my girls with their first feelings of abandonment and loss. Sydney although the youngest did not handle people leaving her even if it was for unforeseeable reasons very well, you could look into her eyes and see that she took it as a feeling of desertion or rejection. My return from the rehabilitation center was a joyful time for all of us, but

Remi being the leader of the pack decided she was laying down the law regarding who could be near me - especially in bed - and poor little Syd, well she was left out in the cold until Remi finally allowed her to be near her mommy.

I think back to my days in the rehabilitation center, and the differences between my girls. Georgia never got to visit, but she was the one who had the pleasure of bringing me home. Remi, she nearly knocked my wheel chair over trying to get in with me then just sat there by my side after she cautiously came through the elevator doors. My little baby Sydney was very young when this happened. Again, it was a fall day; not as warm as when Remi came to visit, but still it was a beautiful sunny afternoon. I was sitting up on the visitors' roof waiting for her to come, hoping once again that she would make the ride like REM REM.

She did not like cars too much either, but then the doors of that elevator room opened and out she pranced. Sydney loves people and she made it a point to say hello to everyone. Then she came to give me a big kiss. She realized she could not sit in my chair, so she sat herself down in front of me looking at me, cocking her head from side to side, trying to size up the situation. Then, looking at the chair, she would kiss my legs, my hands and jump up, kiss me on the mouth again, and go back to sitting and cocking her head with this perplexed look. She would do this over and over again. I think she thought if she did it enough I would get up and walk. Sydney finally got tired and started sniffing around the flowers, looking back at me. She wanted me to walk her in my wheel chair. I responded and we walked (well, I rolled) the perimeter of the roof garden as Sydney explored and said hello to the other patients and their guests. My father wasn't too far away, always watching to make sure that Sydney wouldn't get loose from me and cause a commotion. But she was an Angel that day; very protective, gentile and loving as she walked with the regality of a show dog. I never thought I would see the day when Sydney would be calm on a leash, but she proved to us all how intelligent and sympathetic to my condition she was, even though she was still so young. Upon my arrival at home she had to take a back seat to Remi once again, because REM REM was the leader, and Georgia was the Matriarch. Little Sydney was still the spoiled baby in their eyes, but for those two hours she got to take care of her mommy and prove that she could do it, and she was proud of herself.

Little Syd definitely got the short end of the stick when I came home from the hospital. Georgia would either lie next to me on the floor, or my father would put her in bed with me as my bed was too high for Georgia to climb up. REM REM would lie at the bottom of the bed and every time poor little Sydney would try to get in bed to be near me, Remi would whip around and start ranting. Sydney would try and try to sneak up from all corners of the bed, but Remi would always catch her and start howling like a Mother scolding a child. Sydney would finally give up and just put her head and tail down and either lay on the floor, or slink down the stairs to the couch in the living room. I would feel so bad when she would look back at me with those little eyes but I knew if I did anything to adjust the situation at that time it would just cause more tension between the little pack. Sydney would always find her way back up during the night. She would kiss my hand and I would pet her head and she would go to sleep next to me on the floor or sneak into the bed next to me while REM REM was sleeping. Remi would open her eyes for a moment but she knew that I said it was okay, so she let her in, but she always gave her a stern look. As time wore on and my condition improved Remi finally allowed her back into the bed without "the sneak," and there I would sleep with my three girls; my three Angels.

My husband had left, but we were a family; my father, me and my girls. Remi and Sydney were back to their old selves fighting and playing. They would run circles around each other. Sydney always trying to catch her older sister, and sometimes Georgia would even join in on the fun. You could hear her barking and giving her playful growl when she did; but that devious Syd Vicious, as I liked to call her, because of her mischievous ways, was always looking for that escape route.

They got lucky one day; they thought they were slick. Workmen came to clean our gutters, and when they left they didn't lock the gate. My father let the girls out in the morning while I was at work, but he did not realize that the gate was unlocked. Sydney, on the other hand had the uncanny sense to determine this almost immediately, and with one push, out they went. Georgia stayed behind barking at them as they began their morning excursion. I know this because of what my father told me. He thought Georgia was barking at them or a squirrel, and had no idea that they were on one of their adventures. What they did on their trip is a mystery, and where they went is a mystery. Two or so hours later there was a knock at my house. My father answered it and there was my next door neighbor standing there with Sydney and Remi. Apparently they had finished their exploring and went up and sat on his porch. They thought they had found their way home and were so proud but they missed the house by one. My neighbor told my father he had opened the door to go out, and there they were, just sitting there in front of the door waiting to be let in the house. How long they were there is also another conundrum, but he brought them back to our door to the surprise of my dad, who thought they were playing in the yard the whole time. Where in the world was Georgia? The fear gripped my father as he let the two little ruffians in the front door. Then there was a bark at the back patio doors; the little princess never left the yard. My father let Sweetie Pie in then he went outside to investigate how the terrible twosome got out of the yard in the first place. He locked the gate, and then all three of them went back outside again to play as Georgia barked, giving them both a scolding. They both howled back at her, telling her she was an Old Biddy, and that she had missed all the fun, and they found their way back home anyway.

Life was always interesting in our big house. Sydney was slowly showing how intelligent she was to all. She was also showing how sneaky she could be, and what a little instigator she could be. If she wasn't figuring out ways to escape from the yard digging holes with Remi (which they both were famous for), or bringing Remi with her on adventures, she was learning how to open doors and how to hide things. Hiding things would become one of her favorite past times. Her other favorite thing (like Remi and Georgia) was eventually learning how to stamp her front paws and talk back to her mommy.

My Angels, My Girls

22

SYDNEY GETS A

BOYFRIEND

My husband and I had already split up when he finally stopped fighting me for the girls. He decided to get a wonderful shepherd rotti mix named Aaron. He was, and is, the best natured "big goofy silly boy." My Ex could not have picked a better little boy. The day he brought Aaron over to our house, Sydney's eyes lit up. Remi and Georgia couldn't really be bothered, and I think in the animal kingdom Aaron had it bad for Remi. It was a sin. He would follow her all around but she just didn't want to be bothered. Sydney would follow him around trying to get him to play with her. Eventually that first day they all started playing together, but Aaron's attention was definitely focused on REM REM. Sydney retaliated by being the aggressor in the relationship, and showed him that she liked him in that special way. I am just glad that they both were fixed and that they really couldn't do anything. But Sydney wanted to make her feelings known. What a site to see! It really took Aaron by surprise, and Remi just walked away breathing a sigh of relief. After that, they would all play together, but Sydney and Aaron were quite the twosome. Even to this day, Sydney's eyes light up when she sees her stepbrother, which unfortunately is not very often since her father moved quite a distance away and doesn't come around to see his girls. It's a shame. I really don't think she misses her father since she was so young when he left, but Aaron he is her love.

My Angels, My Girls

23

SYDNEY BRINGS HER

MOMMY A PRESENT

All dogs have the hunter instinct in them; it is ingrained from evolving from wolves. They hunt for survival, food, protection, and in a dog's case, sometimes to please. Studies of dogs and wolves in packs have shown that if a pack member hunted and caught its prey, it would first bring the catch to the head of the pack to show that he or she was subservient to the leader of that pack before it would eat the food. He or she would wait until the leader started to indulge in the food then invite him or her to join out of respect for their status. This is a common practice among pack animals. Sometimes they also have a tendency to fight over live prey if they both catch it at the same time, which is what I believe happened in the case of Georgia and Remi, earlier in my story. Also, at that time my girls weren't really a pack yet, and American Eskimos aren't really "pack dogs," where as Siberian Huskies are. They are closer to their wolf heritage and exhibit more pack, or team behavior.

I broke Georgia and Remi of the hunting spirit that day with the rabbit. Besides not knowing what diseases they could catch by going after and killing another wild creature, I just didn't like the idea of my girls killing another living thing. They could chase them out of the yard, but I did not want them to be killers, so they never did it again. Even Georgia, who out of all my girls was the best watchdog of them all, never did it again.

It was wintertime and Sydney was starting to come into her own. She was getting so smart. She was always vying for my attention and competing with REM REM. She wanted to be the favorite. She still had that baby-runt syndrome in her head. One night it was so cold out you could see your breath. I let the girls out so they could do their business before we went to bed. I called them to come in. Remi and Georgia came in like a flash. Sydney was nowhere to be found. Finally, she came sauntering up the deck steps all pleased with herself. And then she dropped a dead field mouse at my feet. She looked at me with her head held high, tail wagging, her lip curled up in a 'look mommy, look what I brought you, look I saved the house from horrible danger!' smile. She was so proud of herself. I looked down on my family room floor at this frozen mouse carcass. "Oh Sydney, please tell me you didn't kill it." I put the dead mouse in a paper towel; looked at it, made sure she wasn't chewing at it and put it in the trash bin outside. She looked at me, cocked her head, "Mommy did I do something wrong? I just wanted to bring you a present. I wanted to show you I could protect the house." I felt so bad. It's her nature, but all I thought of is the horrible diseases she could have caught by putting that thing in her mouth. She never did it again. I'll always have that picture of her in my mind; Sydney the Huntress. And then how bad that I made her feel even when I tried to explain. Remi let Sydney lay in bed with me that night with no complaints. I think she remembered how she felt when I yelled at her for killing the bunny. I still don't think that Syd killed the mouse, it was too frozen. She wanted to bring it in to me to show me that she could protect the house, and me instead of showing my appreciation and telling her "Good Girl," I got all "mommy" on her, and protective, which is what she was trying to do. She wanted me to be proud of her but instead she almost ended up going to the vet because I was an overprotective mother. Remi and Georgia understood her emotional embarrassment, especially Remi, who went over to her and cleaned her ears while speaking to her quietly. We all went up to bed and Sydney slept quietly in my arms that night. She still was a pup at heart.

My Angels, My Girls

24

SYDNEY'S NEW DADDY

I had separated from the girls' father in June 2002, two months after my first stroke. I told myself that I was not going to let anyone into my life, or theirs, until I met someone special. Someone who wouldn't leave, or hurt my girls, or me. I had been through enough and so had they, and I would not let them go through anything that I could prevent. Finally, in February of 2004 I met someone that I thought was worthy of meeting my girls. Well, Remi and Georgia liked him but they were always a little standoffish and protective. But Sydney always eager and she fell head over heels just like her mother. He would play with Sydney, and once again her eyes came alive. She was so happy! Sydney is a very high-strung, sensitive dog. I think that she took it personally when her father left. She was just two years old and she took it harder than my other girls. I don't think she understood the reasons behind it. He would come over, and she would think he was there to see her. Sydney wanted all of his attention, and he would give it to her. She would sleep between us at night and she felt we were like a family again. Georgia and Remi kept their distance. They would play and observe, but they weren't ready to let anyone in yet. Then just as soon as he was there, he was gone. I was crushed, but Sydney she was devastated. She would mope around the house, worse than when her father left. Then he came back. I was leery of this, but Sydney was happy. Then he did it again. This time Sydney did not mope. She went on a rampage. She tore up things in the trash, had accidents on the floor, barked at me, and destroyed things in my room as if she blamed me for his absence. Her rampage went on for about a week. I couldn't even be angry with her for what she did because I understood what she felt. She felt abandoned. She blamed me for it. I let him into our lives. I trusted his smooth talk. I had promised myself that I would never let anyone hurt my girls, and I let someone right into our home who gained Sydney's trust. Poor trusting Sydney! And he crushed her more than me. At least Georgia and Remi were better judges of character than Syd and I. My dad didn't even see it coming. At first he thought it was nice in the beginning. Syd and I recovered. Unfortunately I kept allowing this person back into my life thinking, "People change," but he hurt my poor Sydney over and over. He was good to Sydney; don't get me wrong, she would love him being there. He was like a father to her, her playmate, and the only male figure I really let around her besides my father (her grandpa). He would come and go whenever things got, as he would say, "too complicated." More like whenever it suited him, because the world revolved around him. He didn't care about anyone else, and that is when Sydney would get hurt or go on one of her tangents. It took me three years, but I finally got out of that emotionally damaging relationship, and I am a better stronger person for it. I feel sorry for him. I don't think he will ever know what it's like to truly love and care for someone. To give without receiving anything in return and respect someone, be there for them even when it is not convenient; then maybe he will be able to have an adult relationship and stop hurting people. Sydney, I think she still misses the "Stinky Man" as we came to nickname him over the years, but she has her grandpa, Georgie, and her Mommy. And maybe someday she will have a Daddy that won't leave, or maybe we will just keep our family just as it is. I know next time I will be a lot more careful of who I introduce to my girls. I will also follow Georgia's lead when it comes to men since REM REM isn't around anymore. Or maybe she'll show up in spirit and drop a drink on them like she did when she was alive.

My Angels, My Girls

25

THE ACCIDENT

My father's accident affected each of my girls differently. Remi automatically became the protector, Georgia the mother, but Sydney was still somewhat of a baby and scared to death of losing someone else that she loved. She was only four and a half when my father first got hurt and she really didn't know what to do, how to react. She just wanted to be near him the same as she wanted to be near me when I had my strokes. The problem with Sydney was she didn't understand that if she jumped on top of my father she could hurt him, and that he couldn't play. She would jump all over his bed trying to play with him. I would be yelling at her Remi and Georgia would be scolding her in their way, and she would get her feelings hurt. Eventually she started to understand, and she would just lay up there in his bed with him and look at him. As soon as he was able to use a walker or a cane she thought he was able to play again and she would bring her ball to him. Then she realized that he couldn't play and she would get very sad and withdrawn. Each time my father would go in the hospital for surgery she would pace. You could see the stress and anxiety continuing to build in her every time.

Things were getting pretty bad. My father was home but almost completely bed ridden, we were packing to move, and Sydney didn't understand what was going on. All these people were coming and going through her house. She didn't like it. She didn't understand why there were so many boxes. I kept working and packing but Sydney would try to unpack the boxes. She thought it was a game.

That May night when Remi died was horrible for all of us. Poor little Sydney didn't believe she was gone. She ran around the house looking for her sister. Remi was like a mother to her. Remi taught her how to be a Husky, and taught her how to talk and howl. She also scolded Syd when she needed it; she showed Sydney the ropes. Sydney was frantic. She was up the entire night. Every time she heard a noise she thought it was Remi. She howled, wailed, and searched for days. It was pitiful. She had finally started to calm down when I brought Remi's ashes home; Sydney was able to smell REM REM's essence through the cedar chest. She went nuts howling, scratching, whimpering, and trying to get into the chest, the poor thing. I didn't know what to do but hold her, and Georgia too; who by this point had started crying, too. I began to cry and howl along with them, the three of us together howling for REM REM. Remi would have been touched and proud to see her sisters, and her mommy howling in unison for her that night, and so many other times after we felt her presence.

26

THE MOVE

All things must come to an end, and it was time to move out of the big house, the only home that Little Sydney ever called home. The past six months had been so trying on her; my father's accident, REM REM's death, and now she had to leave her home. We tried to make it as painless as possible for them; the night before the move my ex-husband came and picked up Georgia and Sydney so that they could stay at his house and not have to deal with all the hustle and bustle of moving day - settlements, lawyers and moving men. I thought that would be the best thing. The day dragged on and on. With moving; one settlement led into another; my quick closings were anything but quick. By the time I got everything settled, including my poor father, it was almost 9:00 that night.

As I reiterate from earlier in the book, I rushed to go pick up the girls from their father's house. I thought that I would have a hard time getting them out of his house since Aaron, Sydney's boyfriend, their stepbrother, and Sydney would still want to play. I knocked on the door, but my ex and his girlfriend were not at home. The door was unlocked, so I went in. Syd and George were so happy to see me, but they were a quiet happy; no jumping, barking, or howling. They just wanted me to put their leashes on and go. I patted Aaron on the head, and off we went to our new home. I never found out what happened when they stayed there that night and frankly I don't want to know, but I know this - they were scared. Sydney was scared; after that day she never wanted to go near her father's house again. If we would go to the dog park near his house she would start howling and crying. If we would get near his house she would calm down after we went by it. Whatever happened in there frightened her. My girls are spoiled, so maybe they got reprimanded too much or they didn't like the girlfriend he had at the time, but whatever it was, they never wanted to go back there again. And I would never take them. But Aaron could come visit us at the new house to play.

Sydney became acclimated to our new house almost immediately, but Georgia had trouble with the hardwood floors. Sydney's problem with the house was that it was much smaller and that the corners were much sharper, so when she would run and take quick turns she would end up sliding into the walls. At just five years old she still had not grown into her big floppy feet, and I don't think she will ever grow into her tongue. She just ran round and round all over the house; up and down, misjudging the turns and sliding into the walls, and she didn't care. Sydney was having a blast getting adjusted to her new digs. I took them outside in the back yard which was so dark I had to put all the lights on in the back of the house to illuminate it, and bring a flashlight just to keep an eye on my Sydney. After all I knew that the fence wasn't too great, and Sydney being master escape artist, I needed as much light as possible back there. Sydney immediately started checking out possible escape routes and I immediately started looking for cinder blocks to plug them up. My Syd Vicious is a terror; but she is also the baby, and all she wants to do is play. She has been through so much already in her young life.

We finally all settled in for our first night at the new homestead. Because of all the unpacked boxes and disarray, we got take out from across the street at the bar and sat in my dad's room, ate and then helped him get ready for bed. Sydney, Georgia and I went upstairs to our new bedroom and went to sleep in the big king size bed amidst all the boxes. I would tackle that in the morning. Unfortunately they wouldn't get tackled for a little while longer due to another round with the insidious infection festering in my father's leg that would rear its ugly head by morning for yet another time. My father woke up screaming. Sydney was first to the scene trying to comfort him, trying to lick his wound; she didn't want anyone to see the bloody mess as she tried to clean it up on the floor. My father and I tried to shoo her away; we didn't want her to get sick. She didn't understand. She thought she was doing good trying to clean everything up and take care of her grandpa. She started whimpering, howling, and pacing. Then Georgia started barking and whimpering. I had no choice but to put them in the yard while I got the doctor on the phone. Sydney was a complete mess, and I had to get my father to the hospital. No need to repeat the entirety of the story - my father was back in the hospital that day - for the next six months. All of our lives changed. Perhaps Sydney's changed the most dramatically; the baby was growing up, or at least trying to grow up.

27

SYDNEY GETS OUT

My father had been back in the hospital for about two weeks. I had suffered a severe contusion of the collarbone, shoulder and concussion from my armoire falling on me while I was trying to put together my stereo system by myself. I am impatient and do too many things on my own instead of waiting for help. Well that incident taught me. Moving forward a couple of days, I needed my lawn mowed and I couldn't pull the starter to get it going because of my injuries. A friend of mine suggested her cousin mow the lawn for me for $30. Well he did a good job until the pull cord broke, and unbeknownst to me left the gate to the backyard wide open when he left. I let Georgia and Sydney outside to play in the yard because they had been stuck in the house for the last two hours, and the next thing I hear is Georgia barking like crazy. I look out back; there is Georgia but where is Sydney? I look to the left - I see that the gate is wide open. At that point there is a knock on the front door and there are these two little girls on the step, "Miss, your dog is down the street." I was frantic. I gave the one little girl the leash to get Georgie, as she was now making it out to the front lawn and out of the gate; to make sure she didn't get away and I asked her to lock up the gate, bring Georgia in, and shut the door as I started screaming for Sydney. Sydney makes an appearance in at the bottom of our block laughing at me. I call to her, she runs to me; then darts to the left of my house. She runs into my next-door neighbor's yard, and with two hops she is three yards away. She runs up again; this time she bolts left. The cement workers are just standing there not doing a thing. You would think they would have helped us try to catch her, but no, they just stood there looking stupid. She thinks it's a game. A dangerous game, as she now makes a right onto a major road. Thank God, she had the sense to stay on the sidewalk. I'm chasing her, calling her name, "Sydney! Sydney you get back here! Please Sydney. Mommy can't do this today!" I'm flying down the street, arm in a sling, high on pain medication, dizzy from the concussion and the heat, and she just keeps running. Every now and then she slows, turns around, stops, and lets me think I'm going to catch up to her - then she is off again. By this point, she looked like the pied piper leading a parade. She was in her glory. I was chasing her with about six kids from the neighborhood and no one could catch speedy. Finally, she turned into an industrial park which could have either been a blessing or a curse; so much machinery, so many buildings, soooo many hiding places and she knew it. But she got scared of all the noisy construction equipment, and she came running right towards us, tongue flapping in the breeze - then we had her. I grabbed her. I hugged her, I kissed her, and then I wanted to smack the living daylights out of her. We got her back on the leash and started our walk home. Sydney was happy as a lark. She had a whole group of new friends that thought she was just "It". Sydney was the leader of the parade of people now walking back to the house. Once back at the house all the kids had iced tea and played with both Sydney and Georgia in the backyard. They had a grand day, and from that day forth the kids came over at least once a week to play with Syd and George. I had met my neighbors and the neighborhood kids that day and realized that my girls would be well protected. I also knew I would never use that guy to cut my grass again, and that I would have to be extremely careful with my little escape artist. This would not be her last attempt at freedom; she is after all a Husky. She may love her mommy, sister, grandpa and home, but she will always love to explore. And unlike Remi she knows no fear, and thinks everything is a game. Sydney is an overgrown puppy who will never grow up.

28

TRANSITIONS

That summer brought with it many changes; my father's re-admittance into the hospital, the loss of my job, the move into the new house, the impending divorce, and Sydney felt all of it. She would lay her head next to me at night. The one thing that we both had, or thought that we both had, was my boyfriend. He had been there to help me set up the house, hang the pictures and offer some emotional support. We were like a little family setting up our new home. Sydney was happy; she always thought of him as her father. He would play with her when he got home and she would cuddle with him - and how she would listen to him. I actually got a little jealous of how well behaved she would be when he was around - almost as if she was trying to impress him so he wouldn't leave us. Georgia the smart one kept her distance and I should have known better.

My father had his final surgery that September. They had managed to correct the damage that had been done by the previous surgeries and infection, and lengthen the leg. We were set to bring him home and the infection started again. No one could understand why or where if it was set so deeply into the bone. My father was sent to another rehabilitation facility. I was running out of hope, on unemployment, just moved into a new house, had a pending divorce, at which point I would lose my health insurance. My one life line, my boyfriend, decided then that things were again getting "too complicated" for him. I was used to it from him. It wasn't like he hadn't done it to me before, but Sydney couldn't handle it this time. She couldn't handle another person leaving her. Her first episode was the most frightening thing I ever saw in my life and I prayed to God Almighty it would never happen again.

It was a couple of weeks when Sydney realized my boyfriend wasn't coming back. She had been agitated and moping; we all had been worried about my father. I had even begun bringing the girls to the rehab to see their grandpa on Sundays. This particular day she was more agitated than usual. Sydney proceeded to jump from one couch to the other like she normally does, but this time she missed and fell between the coffee table and couch. She got up, let out a small little whimper, and tried to shake it off; but she couldn't. She wobbled like a little doe taking her first steps. Then, while trembling, this glazed look of fear overcame her eyes as she lost control of her back legs. Her front paws extended straight out in front of her. She shook for about three minutes. All I could do was stroke and pet her, and keep telling her she was going to be all right. My poor little baby! I knew what seizures were like. I had been through them, and the turmoil they put your body through. Now I watched it happen to my little baby. Georgia was mortified. She just stood there speechless for once, and when Sydney was done, she came over and started kissing her. I immediately called the vet, who told me that seizures are common in Siberian Huskies, and we would have to watch her from now on. She didn't have a full-blown seizure, so it was probably brought on by all the stress that she was under because she was so sensitive. The vet said if it happened again, more frequently, or more violently, she would have to go on medication. My poor baby! I was petrified now. Before I was scared of her getting Bolla like Remi had; now I had to be scared of her having this, especially with her being so sensitive. Still, no one believes how much animals feel. It is beyond my concept of thinking that human beings can be so shallow and plain stupid not to realize how their actions not only affect other human beings but every living breathing soul on this planet - animal or human.

Life went on. Sydney went back to being her playful, sneaky self. It was almost like that horrible day never happened. It was a nightmare that I was hoping to forget. My friend came over one day to work on the electric; he played with Sydney. Sydney was finally getting over her loss and becoming a big flirt and a pick-pocket. All morning, as my friend was working on the electric, she would be stealing his tools out of his pockets, his tool box, and teasing him with what she stole. But then she must have spied his wire cutters and she really liked them. When Sydney finds something she really likes to steal; forget it. She isn't playing and teasing you with it anymore. If she manages to get it away from you, they are hers, and fair is fair. At least that is the way she sees it, and she will hide her prize somewhere you will never expect. Sydney doesn't bury things because she forgets where she buries things, so she hides things in drawers, behind sofa cushions, in cabinets; places that are easily accessible to her. She is smart and knows how to open doors. I just wish she knew how to shut them when she was done! It would save me a lot of bruises. Back to the wire cutters... she thought my friend's wire cutters were so pretty, small with silver tips and blue and gold handles, and they were gone in a flash. My friend and I looked high and low that day for them. We teased her; we even thought that she might have eaten them because they were so small. My friend said. "Well, when she sh*ts them out call me." Sydney just continued to jump around playing, and laughing because she knew where those wire cutters were. My friend left. I told him I'd call him when I found the wire cutters. I found the wire cutters two months later in my father's drawer! She must have opened the drawer and slipped them in there when we were working on my father's room that day. I showed her the wire cutters and she just got this little smirk on her face and tried to take the wire cutters away from me again! After all they were hers; she stole them fair and square and she was proud of herself. Everything is always a game to Sydney.

Everything was going well, she hadn't had a spell in months, and Daddy came home for Christmas but his condition was still worrisome. We all prayed for a miracle. It came and my father was blessed; the infection was held at bay. Our Christmas was lean that year but it was perhaps the best Christmas present we could have received. I was able to finally start looking for work again, which could not have come soon enough since my divorce was now final, and I had to pay for my own health insurance as well as everything else.

My entry back into the work force that February was a happy one for me with a great job. The girls, as I mentioned before in Georgia's story, were not happy, but Sydney my little sensitive one took it as another loss. Each day as she watched her grandpa learn how to walk again with the nurses and the physical therapists; she also watched me leave every morning, and each time I left she had this fearful distraught look that I would not come back. I had been home with her for six months and I would leave for only a couple hours at a time, but now I was gone for nine or ten hours a day again. Oh, she was petrified… I didn't realize how badly things were getting for my playful little girl until I came home one day and the physical therapist was still there with my father. My father had called me to come home from work. The physical therapist told me Syd had had another seizure. "She came running around the corner, then she just stopped and got this glazed look, her front paws went out in front of her, and she kept trying to walk but she couldn't." he said. There she was, laying on the couch in a ball with these sad little rejected eyes, the eyes that I remember seeing when she was a pup in the "On Sale" bin. She looked at me then looked away; she wanted me to know that she felt I abandoned her. I collapsed on the couch with her, started holding her, and cried. My poor little girl, I just wanted to make everything okay. I called the vet again, who said just to monitor her again, and we prayed. Our praying worked for a while. That was only her second seizure, and they were six months apart. Maybe she wouldn't have anymore. We just kept praying.

Sydney went back to her usual self after that day, antagonizing the physical therapists and the nurses. We were blessed that the agency sent us people that were animal lovers. My father even had one nurse who made the mistake of bringing the girls treats when she came. I say that it was a mistake because she didn't realize how much the girls, especially Sydney, would enjoy those treats. And she also underestimated Sydney's pick-pocketing ability. Each time she would come to take my father's blood for his coumadin levels she would bring them doggy biscuits. One day while she was taking my father's blood, her eyes were away from her purse and Sydney's snout was completely immersed inside, finding and then removing the doggie biscuits. Sydney wasn't eating them at the moment; she was saving them for later, stuffing them down the sofa pillows. If she liked something, she'd steal it and hide it to make sure she had it for later. The nurse finally turned and caught her. My father yelled at Sydney, but Sydney just cocked her head and gave the nurse a big kiss, and she laughed. She came back the following week with treats again for the girls, but she was a little more protective of her purse this time. Of course the master thief still tried her best, but when she didn't succeed, the nice nurse gave her extra treats.

29

SYDNEY GETS TRAPPED

I had met my neighbors before on both sides, down and across the street, and fortunately I have been extremely lucky this time around. The people that were living to the left of me unfortunately moved this past summer but when they were living there they were the greatest neighbors one could have. Sydney had already met their kids, as a matter of fact; they were the girls that alerted me to the fact that Sydney was out on her first excursion when we first moved in to our house. The girls and their friends had continuously come over to visit both Sydney and Georgia and they would, sometimes under my supervision, take them for walks. I could never trust Sydney on a walk without me. She is just too crazy and too strong. She would be taking these girls for a walk! The girls though had never met my neighbor's parents.

The fence in the back was in great need of repair, it was falling down in spots, different boards were out it was rotted and dilapidated, it was also connected to my neighbors. My neighbors had a little old dog which became Georgia's barking buddy every night the two of them from the day we moved in would have extensive conversations with each other. Sydney would chime in with her bark-howl, but the conversation mostly would be mouth ol' mighty and her friend back and forth until me or my neighbor would go and get our kids in. My neighbor was afraid that her little dog would have a heart attack because he was getting so old because he and Georgia would really go at it vocally I mean.

Nothing would prepare him, my neighbor or Sydney the day that Sydney decided to visit. The fence was old, the boards were loose. I kept nailing them back into place; I knew that their fence was even worse than my yard, both fences were horrible. They had probably been up for at least 10 to 15 years. This one day Georgia and Sydney were outside playing, I guess it was close to dinnertime when I heard Georgia barking hysterically, I heard my neighbor's dog barking, and then I heard Sydney howling and wailing. "What the heck is going on?" I said to myself as I ran to the back door. I see Georgia running back and forth all along the side of the fence barking like crazy; then I see Sydney peeking out from one of the broken boards thrusting herself into the fence crying, scared to death.

My Angels, My Girls

Somehow Sydney had managed to get herself onto the other side of the fence into my neighbor's yard and now she was trapped there. She forgot how she got in and didn't know how to get back and she didn't like it one bit. The neighbor's dog was barking at her, she was trapped; the genius had no idea what to do. I saw where she had gotten in at and I was scared now if she pushed the fence one way it would lead her back to the safety of our yard but if she pushed the fence the other way she would be out and in her state God knows where she would run she would have access to the busy street where I had almost lost her a year before. I had to think fast, I couldn't understand why no one was coming out from my neighbors; they must have heard all of the commotion. Oh Dear Lord, I thought what if they weren't home. I ran and started banging on their front door. I could hear Sydney still howling and crying in the back...then nothing. Finally, my neighbor opened the front door and through the back with her son ran Sydney safe and sound. My neighbor had been in the shower and her son had just got home they hadn't heard all the commotion, then they looked out and saw Sydney trying to crawl under the fence, whimpering and their dog barking. My neighbor's son went out and fixed the fence that Sydney had pushed through. They were equally worried about their poor little dog getting out the back of the fence and onto the streets. I put Sydney back on her leash as she was now calmed down from her harrowing experience, but was now starting to explore my neighbor's house, which was rather nosey of her, but then that was my demon child. We left my neighbor's house and they of course had fallen in love with her; they thought she was crazy and a goof ball but they loved her all the same. My neighbor now understood why her daughter was so taken with her for the past year and why she was always over my house playing with Sydney and talking about Sydney, Sydney, Sydney. I took Sydney home, stuck her in the bathtub, which was an Olympic feat in itself and gave that girl a bath she was covered with mud and heaven knows what else. By the time we were finished, the entire bathroom was soaking wet but she was clean and happy. Oh, of course, while she was getting her bath Queen Mouth O'l Mighty had to put her two cents in, she had to let Sydney know how upset she was with her and how scared she was when she was trapped on the other side. That was the first and last time I got Sydney into the bathtub for a complete bath.

30

MY LITTLE HEALER

Sydney has always been the most sensitive of all my girls. REM REM was the protector and Georgia was the Matriarch and Queen. Sydney is the baby, the most spoiled, the biggest con artist and probably the most intelligent. Above all she is the most compassionate and good-natured. These two qualities I believe pulled my father through his illness and continue to enrich his life. Sydney and Georgia are both with my father on a daily basis keeping him company and he watches after them, and cleans up after them when they have accidents. They are his life.

My Angels, My Girls

Nothing gives my father more pleasure than watching Sydney play with her ball. She runs around playing by herself tossing the ball in the air, catching it, throwing it, catching it and throwing it again. She has so much fun playing by herself. It is really a shame now that Georgia is older, and with Remi gone she has no one to play with, but that doesn't stop my little Syd. She makes the best of it by tossing that ball around hoping that my father will throw it to her, and also waiting for me to get home to play with her and toss her the ball. She has so much fun playing by herself. She loves to play, she loves to please and she loves to love and take care of others. I found this out all too recently after REM REM died. My little demon child now had taken on the roll of caregiver, not only with her grandfather but also with me. She would kiss away my tears when I was sad, and when I was sick she would lie along side of me as if she was a person. She would wrap her front leg over me and nuzzle her head between my head and neck.

I had major surgery last year and was unable to walk up the stairs. She and Georgia each made their spots near me on the floor by the couch. Sydney would come up and give me kisses and lay her head on my chest and look at me with her sad eyes, let out a little cry, kiss me again then lay back down so she was never to far from my side. A week into my recovery I was able to venture back upstairs to my bedroom for the rest of my recovery, and Sydney was not far behind. If she was not lying in the bed beside me, she would come upstairs for her hourly check ups and kisses, and to make sure that I was doing okay. Sydney had become my little baby Angel. Yes, she can still get herself into trouble but she has become the most sensitive, loving and caring little four-legged child I have ever laid eyes on. Quite a difference from the backward little ruffian in that "On Sale" crate all those years ago.

That summer I finally put in the new fence. I thought, "Finally, I don't have to worry about her getting out." But by the time I got home that day she had the place cased and had already started working on her escape tunnels. My ground wasn't exactly, or should I say, was extremely not level and she found every spot where that fence was not close to the ground, or where there was already a hole in the ground from the previous fence that wasn't filled in well. The contractors tried to plug up what they could; they used old railroad ties where it was particularly bad, but that little stinker she found every spot that wasn't plugged up. It was reminiscent of Remi and Georgia years before with dirt from their heads to their toes from digging. Out I went with cinderblocks, bricks, and anything I could get to plug up those holes; Syd behind me trying to move the blocks, howling, talking away, giving me looks. Oh yeah, Sydney is one for throwing some nasty looks when she is mad at you or not getting her way, then with a huff she'll just walk away and ignore you, She has gotten really good at that too. I think she had learned that from Georgia because REM REM could never hold that sulking spoiled baby thing. Georgia was a champ at it but Sydney might actually be about ready to take over that championship as she gets older. They both know how to con their mother; that is definitely for sure.

Summer came and went, everyone was doing good now, my dad was doing better, Georgia's hair was slowly growing in Sydney hadn't had a seizure in over six months, I had recuperated from my surgery and was back to work at the same job; I was lucky they hadn't let me go. I had only been there a few months when I had taken ill, so I had a lot to be grateful about. I even decided to give my boyfriend another chance; the third time is a charm is what they say. Syd was happy, she loved him. I think she liked the way he smelled when he came home from work, so unbeknownst to him the nickname of the "Stinky Man" was still used when he wasn't around. All you would just say to Sydney "Where's the Stinky Man?" she would just jump out of her skin, wagging her tail and run all around the house looking for him, everywhere that he would usually be, then she would sit at the door waiting. Oh, she was happy. I don't know, maybe Sydney's disposition had the capability to emotionally heal everyone - maybe even relationships. She would make everyone happy and laugh even if she was being annoying and incorrigible.

Life was finally good. We were moving into the Christmas Season, I was having my first poem published, and everything was coming up roses. We couldn't wait to usher in Christmas and the New Year. That Christmas I was going to spoil my girls rotten to make up for the past few holidays when they basically got rooked when money was tight or there just was too much drama, turmoil, and sadness in our little home. Above all, I was finally going to take Sydney to see Santa. She had never been to see Santa Clause and she had already turned six. It was something that had been a tradition for Georgia and Remi, but because of all the turmoil in our home Sydney never got to experience it. Sydney never even experienced a trip to Pet Smart. We were always afraid because she was so excitable and friendly that people would take it the wrong way. To be frank, a lot of people do not understand that animals are just trying to be friendly. I guess I am over protective of my girls and I keep them in the yard mostly because of this.

31

A PERSONAL NOTE TO

SOCIETY

I've worked in Personal Injury law for a long time. And I've seen lawyers monopolize cases on the issue of dog bites. Sometimes it is the animal, true— but most of the time the animal is the defenseless one. It was either preyed upon by horrible owners that trained it to be vicious, or most often than not, the poor dog was tormented by some wise-assed kid who kept pulling its tail or its ear or something else, or poking at it or taunting it or bullying it until the poor dog (or even cat) finally turns around and bites or scratches the kid. Or sometimes it is a plain and simple accidental scratch. The parents get sued and the poor dog or cat, most of the time a lovable dog who just wants to play, will end up being put down, or end up in a shelter kept away from their family, wondering what they did wrong. And then they will start biting and defending themselves because they became scared of human beings. The child or adult that put them there? What happens to them? Nothing. Not a thing. If the child did that to another child they would be grounded or maybe be required to see a psychoanalyst, but because it was an animal, society blames the dog.

Yes, I put my political views into my book. You can agree or disagree, but I will tell you one thing; I know my girls are very loving and playful and I am extremely careful who I allow near them. I would never want Sydney to be accused of attacking a child because she jumped on them to try to give them a kiss, or Georgia being accused of attacking a child because she showed her teeth. She has never bitten anyone in her life because a child pulled her tail. We live in a very litigious society. After hearing what happened to a poor dog in this one town that was put down because he attacked a boy, even when everyone knew this boy taunted the dog, and that it was not the fault of the dog. He was just playing with the boy's dog. The judge did not want to put him down, but unfortunately after being locked away from his family in a shelter for a long period of time, and the boy taunting that dog, and the other dogs in the shelter when he would come visit his dog, from being locked in the shelter the dog finally bit a shelter worker. So in the judge's ruling he had to put the dog down because there was something wrong with him. Before this incident everyone stated that the dog was the friendliest dog, and before this had never harmed a fly. People say that prisons change people and it doesn't take a rocket scientist to figure out that this poor innocent dog was taken from his family after being taunted by this boy and continuously taunted while he was in the shelter and kept from his family. What do you think happened to the dog? He was scared, scarred, abandoned, and depressed. Hey, I'm human, and if I was locked up for defending myself and kept away from my family and being taunted every day, I would be biting the shelter keeper too in that situation. But that's just me. I sometimes wonder if anything was done with the boy; if he was required to under go any psychiatric evaluation, or if he feels any remorse at all. That's society BLAME IT ON THE DOG! Heed the warning; protect your four-legged kids. Always have them on a leash, keep them close, and watch who you allow into their lives and even into your homes. It may sound cynical but you never know who may be out for a quick buck off you, and your precious pet.

Another thing comes to mind. What about these people, or should I even call them people because they are lower than scum, that organize dog fights. Some of them even cut the ears off of the dogs... it's disgusting. What is their punishment? Maybe a few years? If they did that to a human being they would be going up the river for a lot longer than that, wouldn't they? These people need to be stopped. Society needs to be shown that animal cruelty is not acceptable behavior. Their sentences need to be stiffer and they are the ones that need to be chastised and boycotted. Stick them in a ring with their ears cut off and let them fight to the death. Darn, I have to stop voicing my political views and stay on point. This is a family book about my babies after all. Now, back to my Sydney.

32

SYDNEY GETS TO SEE

SANTA, FINALLY

The day finally arrived! Santa was at Pet Smart. I didn't know how I was going to handle both Sydney and Georgia with the lines, and Sydney's unruliness. The morning started bright and early. They both had to be primped and groomed by a new groomer. This should be interesting. Neither of them had been to a groomer since we had moved to our new neighborhood. I loaded them into the car first thing in the morning and off we went. Georgia sat in the front seat looking out the window like the Queen Bee and Sydney roamed all over the car howling like a maniac. She never liked driving in cars; it must be a husky trait. Remi had hated it too. The new groomer seemed nice, and the shop was homey. Sydney tried to steal the treats off the counter as soon as we walked in, so of course they had to put on their act and start crying and hiding behind their mommy's legs when it was their turn to be taken back. Sydney the big baby and con artist would always make me feel like she was being led down that last mile whenever I left her anywhere. Luckily, the groomers were quick. They called me within two hours, which for dog groomers is fantastic. I picked them up; they both looked adorable with their little Christmas bandanas on, and they each had a bag of treats that the groomer gave them as Christmas presents. My little Sydney Sue looked especially pretty.

She actually looked black and white again instead of black, brown and grey. I piled them into the truck and we went home. As I was driving I thought to myself, "How am I going to do this Santa Claus thing with them?" I decided the easiest thing to do was to take one at a time, and leave the other one at home. We arrived home, and Sydney - who is always quick to jump out of the car first - I trapped with my arm. She was not pleased as I pushed her back into the back seat and grabbed Georgia and made a quick getaway to the house leaving Syd in the car. She was screaming like a banshee as I ran up to the front door of our house, opened it, and made the hand off to my father. The whole exercise must have taken a total of 30 seconds; enough to aggravate Baby Syd, who by this point was jumping and howling all over the inside of the car because she hates being confined. But we were on our way. Sydney was going to finally see Santa.

We pulled up to the Pet Smart parking lot and it was packed, but luckily it was early. Santa had just started taking pictures with the pets. I had a little talk with Sydney before we even got out of the car, asking her to please behave, and not jump on anyone, but she had this funny look in her eyes as she looked at all the people and all the other dogs. My little Syd Vicious; the crazy girl, the goof ball, Miss energetic instigator, was actually timid. Maybe it was the excitement of the day, the early morning groomer appointment with so many other dogs, and now this experience, and Georgie not there to show off for and back her up... I don't know but she started to whine. I was so worried about her getting away from me in the store and causing a commotion, yet she was so sweet and quiet. She shyly walked along side of me. If people approached her she meekly looked up at them, let them pet her, sniffed their hand and maybe kissed it. There was no jumping, no barking, howling, running, pulling or butt and crotch sniffing. I was looking at her with the puzzled look of "Who are you and, where is my Sydney????" I thought of the movie "Invasion of the Body Snatchers" because this was definitely not Sydney.

It was finally our turn to see Santa. Sydney was usually a ham in front of the camera but would not sit still. She was scared to death of Santa and started to cry. Remi used to be scared of Santa too when she was alive, but never this bad. The photographer tried toys, treats; everything in her bag of tricks, but nothing would get Sydney on Santa's lap long enough for the shot. She was little crybaby that day. I finally had to get in the shot with her and Santa, and I was not happy because I was definitely not dressed or made up for pictures that day. But then what can you do? We finally got the shot; Sydney, Santa and me. We left the store; Sydney practically walking between my legs, she was so scared. Me still wondering if I had the right dog; if the pod people had taken her while she was at the groomer. Then, once we got home she was back to herself. That was Sydney's first experience with Santa. I hope this year things will be better. Maybe I'll find a less crowded place to take her.

Christmas 2006 was wonderful. Both my little girls were extremely happy. They each had presents galore, their grandpa was home, and Sydney's "Stinky Man" was there too. Everything was in place; we were a happy family once again. We could feel Remi's presence watching over us as we lit a candle by her picture, and brought out her collar once Stinky Man went to bed because he wouldn't understand. Not too many people would, but this was our way of including her and remembering her. After our moment of remembrance for Remi, the girls both went back to their own thing. Sydney was tearing apart more and more presents. She was less interested in the treats and more interested in the toys. She will always be an overgrown puppy. She soon found her favorite ball and she ran around the house the rest of the night, tossing it up in the air and catching it. Sydney can always amuse herself. She wishes Georgia would play with her, but she knows that if she persists too much Georgia will give her the ol' growly growl, so she has learned to amuse herself and she does a great job. Sydney has a side to her that is endearing but annoying, and drives my little sweetie pie Georgie nuts.

My Angels, My Girls

33

SYDNEY THE NUTTER

From the time she finally started to feel comfortable in our house, Sydney always had to be first. First in the door, first out the door; it didn't matter where or how, she was going to be first and she was going to run over anyone to get there, including poor little Georgie. When REM REM was alive she was a bit calmer because Remi, of course was the leader of the pack, but now forget about it, all bets are off. She will run over everybody: Georgia, me, her Grandpa; she always thinks she is missing something. However, the second you yell at her, tell her no, or she realizes she stepped on Georgia or me, or heaven forbid, her grandfather, the tail automatically goes down and she comes back whimpering, kissing your boo boo. She knows that she isn't supposed to do that but she gets so excited she'll do it again and again and apologize in her way again and again. Torturing Georgia has become her favorite thing to do in life. She loves to play, and Georgia is just getting too old. Sydney will go out in the yard at least 10 times a day by herself, but when Georgia accompanies her she runs around, well... like a NUTTER. Round and round she goes trying to get Georgia to play; biting her head, and jumping back and forth over top of Georgia. On the rare occasions that Georgia gives in, it's a site to see. It brings me back to the old days when REM REM was alive, with them chasing each other around the yard.

Georgia barking and growling at Sydney in a playful way.

The most playful time for both of them is during the first snow. Sydney is at her happiest then because Georgia actually remembers what it is like to be a puppy again. They both love the snow. Typical snow dogs! As soon as we get the first decent snow that lies, they are out there romping, rolling, playing, and burying each other in it. I can't get them in the house. Even Georgia at that point, but it's hard for the old girl to make it up and down the deck steps, and I usually have to end up bringing her in. I remember last year the snow came so quick and it was like ice and Sydney wasn't prepared. She went running off of the deck and took a flying leap into the middle of the yard - all four legs straddled about - head right into the snow. I was so scared that she got hurt, but at the same time all I could do was laugh. She looked like a cartoon character. She got up, looked around, shook it off and tried catching snowflakes in her mouth, running around just like a human child would do. Then she would just lie down and roll around in it until she was completely white with her piercing blue eyes sticking out. Then she would come in and shake it off all over the house with a smirk on her face. She thought she was hilarious.

Sydney's most favorite game of them all is king of the mountain. She will stand at the top of the stairs when Georgia is trying to come upstairs for bed at night and not let her. Georgia will move to one side of the stairs - Sydney will go there - Georgia will move to the other - there will be Sydney - she will keep smacking Georgia with her paw on the top of the head. Or race back and forth up and down the stairs while Georgia is trying to walk up. Yes, she has even tried this little game with me on one or two occasions, but her mother always wins so she has given up. She knows she can always intimidate Georgia until her mommy intervenes, then she runs away and comes back kissing Georgia trying to get back into her good graces. After all, she was only playing, and she loves her sister Georgia. Georgia gets sick and Sydney is right there putting her two cents in making sure I'm taking care of her properly. She will lie next to her sister and watch after her like she does for her grandpa, and me. No one sheds a tear around Sydney without her taking care of them, that is definitely for sure, nutter or not.

My Angels, My Girls

34

SEASONS CHANGE

Christmas season had passed. It brought the first snow, and worst ice storm since 1994. Things were starting to change for us again in this New Year. My boyfriend, a.k.a. "the stinky man," was starting to act strange again so I decided once and for all I was going to slowly delete him from my life for good this time. Starting with him moving out of my house. This had to be a gradual procedure considering the reaction it had on Sydney when he abruptly left in the past. So this time it had to be done slowly. I knew he was up to no good but I had to think of Syd and slowly break up with him so he would be out of our lives for good this time. This was worse than going through my divorce. Sydney had become so attached to her lovable favorite stinky man...

35

SYDNEY MEETS MY CO-WORKER

I was having a problem with my health insurance last winter; they wouldn't pay for one of the medications that I needed to be on since my stroke. Or should I say it was a miscommunication between the pharmaceutical company that administered the prescriptions and the health insurance not getting it right. Well, because of their miscommunication I ended up in the hospital with a complicated migraine. The doctors did not want to take any chances that it wasn't another stroke (given my history) so they kept me there for quite a few hours, and of course in the end, they had to administer some heavy-duty medication to break the migraine. Considering this episode happened at my office, to get me home that night, my boss and two of my co-workers had to drive me home that evening. Once we arrived at my home my one co-worker had to use my bathroom, which I didn't mind, but that meant he had to meet the family. He came in, introduced himself to my father; patted Georgia and Sydney on the head and proceeded to the facilities. He did his business, came out and continued his conversation with my father. With that Sydney saw her chance to get to know him a little better. She went right up to his crotch to familiarize herself with him and give him a proper hello the way she saw fit. Needless to say, my co-worker was completely surprised and embarrassed.

Sydney was pleased with herself. She felt she had done nothing wrong; after all, that was how she said a proper hello. On the other hand, although I was quite embarrassed, I had a small chuckle to myself at the look on my co-worker's face as he excused himself from our house not knowing what to do. I don't think he ever had something like that happen to him. The next time he had to drop me off at home, he skipped the bathroom. I think that my little Syd Vicious had made a lasting impression on him. He did not want to get goosed again!

It was not long after I had made the stinky man leave that Sydney had another seizure. This was by far her worst seizure yet. It had been a year since her last one. I thought that they were done, and only stress related, but this one was a full grand mal. I was so frightened for my poor little baby. I called the vet after it happened and she told me to watch her. It could be an isolated incident. We wouldn't start her medicating yet, but would just watch her. It has been a year since her last one. I was hoping that it was just the adjustment of the stinky man not being there every night, and the fact that I was hospitalized for a day. Maybe she was just a little stressed out. I prayed that was all it was.

The next day after her spell, Sydney was back to her normal self -tormenting the world. Driving Georgia and my father nuts, counter surfing in the kitchen; back to being Sydney. Stinky man was only coming over once a week now, and then it became every other week, until I finally told him not to come over anymore. Sydney didn't appear to skip a beat. I think she was numb to it this time. She was happy as a lark when he would come over but I think she sensed it, that beginning of the end. She knew that it was only a matter of time before she was never going to see him again.

Unfortunately, Sydney's seizures were not caused by stress. Like most Siberian Huskies she was predisposed to epilepsy. The day we realized Sydney had epilepsy was one of the most horrifying days of my life. I had come home from work one evening, and Sydney who is normally affectionate was so overly affectionate I didn't understand why. I kept thinking she had done something wrong. She wanted to sit in my lap, and Sydney is a little big for a lap dog. She just wanted me to hold her. Then Sydney got up and started to wretch, she started to run from me, wrenching the whole time. Finally she threw up. Her vomit was clear, like bile. She scurried to the back deck doors. I chased after her and let her out. She darted outside and started to pee, then her back legs started to wobble, and then it happened. She fell over on her side, her entire body started shaking, and her jaw clenched shut, her eyes completely rolled back in her head. I didn't know what to do. I just sat next to her, stroking her head. This lasted for about 30 seconds but felt like an eternity. She opened her eyes, kissed my hand and started to get up. She was unsteady and then down she went again, more violent than the first time. "Oh My God, "Sydney!" I screamed. I was crying and stroking her as she lay there helpless in the grass, her body convulsing. My mind was racing. "Please God let her be okay, this is my baby. Don't take her from me!" After what seemed to be another eternity, she finally stopped. Sydney opened her eyes. She looked so listless, she couldn't move. She just continued to lay there in the grass staring into space. I just kept petting her, trying to keep her comfortable, trying to get her to come out of it, praying that she was okay, and trying not to let her see how upset I was. Finally, after about five minutes, I picked her up - all 50 pounds of her - she was like dead weight. I carried her to the door of the house, and just as I was opening the door she started seizing again right in my arms. My little girl was so stiff, every one of her muscles was rigid but she was twitching uncontrollably and all I could see was the whites of her eyes. I got her in to the house and I laid her down on the couch and just petted her until she came out of it. Thank God she did. I called the vet who told me she had gone through a cluster seizure fit and that it was definitely time to start treating her for epilepsy. I went to the veterinarian to get the Phenobarbital for Sydney and we started immediately that night. The Doctor said that if she were to have another one that night she would have to go to the animal hospital and have the medicine given to her intravenously, because cluster seizures can be extremely serious. Luckily God heard our prayers and as soon as we administered the oral Phenobarbital, the seizures stopped. However, when Sydney came out of her cluster seizure fit she was very disoriented. She drank a ton of water and was very helpless. That was probably one of the last times she spent the whole night in bed with her mommy.

36

THE SIDE EFFECTS

The Phenobarbital has helped. Syd has not had a seizure since she has started her treatment, and hopefully she will never have another again. The medication has not been a great experience for her or us. In the beginning, the dosage was too strong and my poor baby was walking around completely out of it, with her legs all wobbly. She would just look at me like she wanted to cry. Once the dosage was corrected she was almost back to herself, but other problems had developed. Sydney, who finally was housebroken after six years, now had an accident almost every night. She cries, whimpers and is constantly agitated, walking and pacing. On the downside she just lays around all day. She has developed what the doctors call "false hunger" and is constantly hungry so we have to watch how much she eats or she will eat herself sick. She doesn't like to sleep in bed with her mommy anymore because it's cooler downstairs. Either that or she is embarrassed about her peeing problem and doesn't want to wake anyone up in the middle of the night, because when she pees in the middle of the night it's a flood. The worst thing of all is that sometimes she will be sleeping and not realize she's peeing then she cries when she realizes it.

I spoke to the vet about her peeing and her mood swings and she immediately ran more blood work. The blood work showed some abnormalities which brought back the fear that maybe it wasn't epilepsy at all. Her seizures may be being caused by the dreaded Cushings Syndrome. Sydney was packed off for another full day of excruciating testing just like sweet little Georgie had gone through so many times in the past. My poor little baby! The day I had to take her in and lead her down the steps of the Animal Hospital, she kept looking at me, "Why, Mommy, Why?" She let out slow, drawn out, little whimpers. The vet technician told me it would be easier if I put her in the cage. I never felt so horrible in my life; putting little Sydney Sue in that cage and taking off her leash. I kissed her little snout and closed the cage, and she was grasping at the metal bars, howling and whimpering which soon became a loud, ear-piercing wail. I left my baby - my little girl with the abandonment issues - I left her in a cage. Although it was for her own good, and she was in good hands. It's not like I haven't left her at the vet's office before for her surgery when she was a pup, or for her x-ray one time before; but that was all before REM REM's death and grandpa's accident. And before her anxiety disorder became so extreme. I walked up the stairs listening to her heart wrenching cry. I knew I would be back to get her that afternoon, but Baby Syd didn't know and she was horrified. I came back later that day to pick her up and I could hear her howling downstairs. The doctor said she did fine and she wasn't a problem, but the vet tech rolled her eyes. I knew who to believe. My little girl didn't get the name Baby Syd for being quiet in the vet's office. Now it was time to go home and begin the praying, bargaining and soul searching. The "what ifs" and the "what am I going to do" same as what I went through with Georgia two times before. Praying for a miracle, praying that it was only congenital epilepsy. What a thing to pray for;

please God let it only be congenital epilepsy! Don't let it be Cushings or a tumor. Two days went by, and finally the results were in; it wasn't Cushings. We had dodged another bullet. We could put her on a medication for the peeing but after reading the side effects that went along with the prescription. I decided she was on enough medication. I would rather clean up her accidents than have her sick from more medication. My little girl had been through enough. Days and days went by, and Sydney soon became more and more like herself. The incontinence continued, although not as frequent and her demeanor was more like the old Sydney, as she went back to tormenting Georgia. Regarding her eating however; well she now has the nickname of Old Hollow Leg, so we still have to watch her on that. I miss her sleeping with me, but she comes up in the morning now and gets in bed with us. I'll say to her as she's creeping around the bed in the early morning light and I hear her collar jingle, "I see those ears, what you doin' Syd, Come On, jump in the beddy bye with Mommy and George!" Up she would jump, do her little dance like most dogs do; it must be three times, then plop herself down in a ball with her head sharing her mommy's pillow, looking right at me, and give me a big kiss on the mouth. That's my Syd; my sweet baby Syd.

37

SYDNEY REMEMBERS

It was an ultra hot day in May. Sydney was still undergoing her testing and going to the veterinarian at least once a week. We pulled into the parking lot at the Animal Hospital. It was packed with cars. I finally found a spot on the end and parked. Sydney was always in a rush to get out of the car and barreled over me trying to get out of the front seat. Luckily I always had her by the lead. Sydney led the way to the door of the office as she normally did; she liked meeting the other dogs in the waiting room and liked playing and talking with them. Being the social butterfly that she is, this was an outing for her. She just didn't like it when it was time to go into the Doctor's office for her appointment. This particular day was different. The office was just too crowded. There were cats, puppies, kittens, and people sitting outside on the steps. I couldn't believe that she had over-booked the appointments like this, unless the poor animals were really sick and needed to get in right away. We went in to the reception desk just to give Sydney's name and to tell them we would be outside. I figured the best thing to do was to take Sydney for a walk. She already had started barking, howling and whimpering; which I did not understand at all. She usually loved all the attention and being the Bell of the Ball. Sydney and I went outside and she was fine. We walked and played, she had some water, she thought she was smart and tried to drag me down the hill; everything she loves to do when we are waiting at the Animal Hospital. We stayed outside and waited for about 30 minutes or so then we went to the front door.

We started to walk in and there he was a big rottweiller-shepherd mix that looked exactly like her stepbrother Aaron. Sydney kept trying to play with him and get his attention but he ignored her. She realized that it wasn't Aaron and she got so upset that she started howling and whimpering again. I had to take her out of the office again, and as soon as I did she would be fine. She would look up at me with these sad confused eyes, and all she wanted to do was go home. She kept heading for the car, so there we sat in the car with a little thing of water as she sat there sulking. Licking her emotional wounds, still confused, part of her still thinking this dog was her brother, but realizing he wasn't. She missed her brother that she loved so much and hadn't seen for so long. I'm sure it had made her think of her father too, the stinky man and the big one REM REM. My poor little sensitive Syd, all those that she had loved were no longer in her life. She is truly the most human of all my angels, and sadly the most emotional. She truly wears her heart on her sleeve. We finally went to the door of the office again. As soon as we opened the door, he was still there; she started crying again, so we turned around and came out. Syd and I sat on the steps until Aaron's doppelganger went into the examination room, then my little baby and I went into the reception room to wait our turn where she played with the other dogs that were also still waiting for their turn.

I've often thought of calling her father. He hasn't visited the girls in over a year. It would be nice for him to bring Aaron over to play with Syd. She really loved Aaron so much. We all did; actually, he was an angel in his own right. I must mention that to Syd, he was her everything; her brother, playmate, the love of her life. She had a serious case of puppy love for that Aaron. Yes, I often thought of asking their father to come for a visit and bring Aaron, but after seeing the suffering she went through in the Animal Hospital that day, and the pangs of abandonment she felt afterward wondering when and if she would ever see her friend again, or her father - it's been over a year for both - maybe it should be a distant memory. I was petrified what would happen when I finally took a vacation this year. She was too young to really remember my being away for so long with my stroke and at least she could visit me there.

38

MOMMY TAKES A

VACATION

I haven't had a vacation in over six years. My stroke, my divorce, my father's accident, moving and Remi's death did not afford me the luxury of taking a little more than a night somewhere - if I was lucky. This was going to be the summer. I made plans with a good friend of mine to go to South Beach; to see the turquoise waters of beautiful Miami, to stay at one of the best hotels with unbelievable views, incredible service and rooms, and to see some old dear friends.

My Angels, My Girls

And let us not forget to mention the restaurants, shopping and night life! There was only one catch; what was I going to do with my father and my girls? I was so afraid to leave them. I could leave them for a night, maybe even two, but this was five, and Sydney - most of all - what was she going to be like? My father's doctor's said he would be fine as long as I had someone looking in on him and that he wasn't alone the whole five days. The vet told me that Sydney would be fine with my father and that she has her mother wrapped around her little finger. Imagine that, you think!! I knew Georgia would be okay; she is my little trooper. So what's a mother to do? Call on Super Nanny! Also known as my close friend, Auntie Jane.

Auntie Jane came for the middle three days to take care of my brood, and to keep me from pulling my hair out in worry. She made sure that my father didn't live off a diet of tasty-kakes, donuts, and ice cream, and that my girls had treats galore, and didn't miss a beat or their mommy, or destroy the house. Because grandpa lets them get away with murder (even more than their mommy) or that they would be living on the donut diet too. On Auntie Jane's first day she took Sydney aside and said, "Your mommy will be back in a few days. Until then I'm all you've got beside your grandpa and Georgia. You need to be good. There will be no peeing or pooping or messing up this house while I'm here." Sydney cocked her head at her, and the next morning at 6:00 am, she came upstairs and woke Auntie Jane up to take her outside. There was no peeing or messing up of the house while I was gone, and the girls had a good time with their Nanny. So did my dad, who said he didn't need anybody to take care of him while I was gone. They all ate and had a good time, and Sydney behaved like the little angel that she can be, and so did Georgia the queen. Sydney though, the demon child at heart, and spoiled rotten to the core, had plans for her mommy. I could tell it in her bark when I called from Miami.

The day I came home from Miami everyone was ecstatic. Sydney was running around like a bat out of hell, Georgia was barking like crazy. They both were running over me. Sydney was jumping on top of me, kissing me, knocking me down. It brought me back to when REM REM was alive and I would come home from trips. They were both nosing all around my suitcase; they knew there were treats and presents in there for them. Mommy wouldn't dare walk into the house after five days and not bring them something. They waited patiently, or should I say semi-patiently for me to slowly unpack my suitcase. I wasn't lugging the heavy monstrosity upstairs. It's amazing how much you accumulate on a vacation. I was shocked I didn't get charged an extra weight fee. Special thanks to the nice Sky Cap at the airport. Sydney paced and paced by my suitcase. She kept sticking her nose in it and looking at me, "Come on Mom, I'm dying over here." "Where are my presents?" Finally, I opened the bag with their presents, gave them each a chewy treat which they both started to mangle then out came the toys. Mr. Seahorse for Georgia - which I laid by her front paws - she laid her head down on it and wagged her tail. And for Sydney, a big squeaky Mr. Iguana. She immediately started running around the room tossing it in the air grabbing it and thrashing it around, then the spoiled child wanted Mr. Seahorse she always has to have everything and so she started to stare Georgia down. Georgia wasn't ready to give up Mr. Seahorse; she wanted it as a pillow. The argument between the sisters began. They never fight, but they argue. Georgia will give the old growly growl and her nasty bark, and Sydney will bark and howl, but that is as far as it will go until one of them gives up. Usually I step in and take all the toys away because I don't feel like listening to them. That was the case that night. I took the toys and put them aside, gave them both more chewy treats, and everyone was happy. The next morning Sydney had both toys and Georgia couldn't care less; it was just that the night before I had given it to her and she wasn't letting Sydney take it until she was good and ready. With that I was off to work, not realizing that Sydney still was not done with her mother yet. My little demon child just gave me a look as I walked out that door behind those mischievous eyes. "Leaving again, are we mommy? I don't think so, I've had quite enough of your leaving" She side-eyed me as I left. Oh, I knew she was up to something. I should have locked my doors to my bedroom but I thought, "I'm safe my father is home. She can't do too much damage." I came home that evening and to my pleasant surprise everything was safe and well. My girls were happy to see me. We played and we went to bed early. Everything seemed fine. Sydney my darling, being the cunning little one that she is, was still in her planning stages. She wanted to enact her revenge on her mother slowly, and it started Friday morning with a bang.

I awoke Friday morning to a distinct smell that I hadn't smelled in my house, especially in the upstairs quarters of my house in a very long time. The smell of DOGGIE POO! Georgia can't jump out of bed to have an accident in the middle of the night, but if Sydney has to have a bowel movement she always wakes someone up unless she is sick, then she will come get you and cry. This was deliberate. Two large logs right at the top of the stairs and Sydney had this huge smirk on her face. "Poo on you mommy! Go away and leave us for five days, then go right back to work and not spend any time with us! I'll show you." After I yelled at her for her little accident or should I say her deliberate act of civil disobedience all appeared to be fine. After all I knew it was coming didn't I? I went on to my day at the office. It was a beautiful day and I decided to take my father out for dinner that evening when I came home - nothing spectacular - just a quick bite after I came home from work. I thought that he had shut the door to the upstairs when I picked him up for supper. I was wrong. Sydney and Georgia now had complete access to the entire house, including my bedroom while we were out having our dinner. This normally would not have mattered, but considering the circumstances of my just coming back from my trip this was not a good thing… not a good thing at all.

It was dusk when my father and I returned home from dinner. I had left the light on in the living room and since it was Friday evening I left the Sci-Fi channel on for Sydney. She liked that channel on Fridays otherwise it would be the Discovery Kids channel. My strange ones do not like Animal Planet like most dogs.

It was a beautiful evening, my father and I had a nice dinner but he was worried when we pulled up. "Did you leave a light on for the girls? It looks dark in there." "Yes, Dad I flicked on the living room light and changed the TV channel on the way out." "Did you shut the door to the upstairs?" Well, it didn't matter at that point, we were home now so we opened the door and there were my angels laying in the living room watching their TV, good as gold, waiting for their supper; or so I thought... My father started to divide the doggy bags between the two of them; I decided to go upstairs to change. I noticed Sydney's little smirk as I began to walk up the stairs, I turned the corner of the stairs and entered the hallway approaching my bedroom then I saw it - my demolished bedroom. Sydney had finally taken her revenge. She pulled every dirty piece of vacation clothing out of the dirty clothes bin and had it strewn all over the bedroom. She tore open every bag of souvenirs that she could find, and she must have heard the car pulling up just has she began chewing on the box of chocolate cigarillos that I had purchased for their Auntie Jane. Oh she had made a mess. She didn't destroy anything except for paper and plastic bags, but she wanted her feelings known.

She wanted me to know that she was not happy that I left her for five days, went right back to work and then had the audacity to go out with her grandpop and leave them both completely alone. Yes, that is my Sydney, my little Syd Vicious the demon child, spoiled rotten little baby. What can you do? I could send her to obedience school or call in the Dog Whisperer, but I love her just the way she is. She isn't going to stop me from going on vacations or going away. She will have to learn this was only the first time, and she will have to grow up and learn to like it.

Two weeks later I was off again. It was only for a night this time. I left in the morning and was back late the next day. Her grandpa was with her, and of course Georgia too. She just gave me the evil eye but when I came home she was all hugs and kisses. She is getting used to it. Sydney is even getting back into the Mommy and Sydney groove again. She is my little sweetheart.

Yes, I will admit it I am ruled by my little girls. They are spoiled and I really don't care because they deserve it for all of the joy, happiness and companionship they have brought my father and me. I am forever in God's debt for bringing them into my life.

39

THE ADVENTURES OF

SYD & GEORGE

I have written about the adventures of Sydney and Remi, yet to this day I still quite don't know how they pulled it off. Sydney and Georgia's adventures mostly take place in the house with Sydney tormenting Georgia, and Georgia retaliating. But to my dismay there have been one or two times when they got out that I did not know what to do, and like the two stubborn little children I wanted to errrgggh. Well, let's just say they get walked one at a time now, and I make sure one is locked in the yard before I take the other one out so they don't know what is going on.

I was taking them both out for a walk one evening, and Georgia decided she couldn't go anymore. She plopped herself down on the front lawn and wouldn't budge. I walked Sydney back into the house and took her leash off, and went out to get Georgia who was still sitting there. Sydney saw a cat and pushed open the door and went flying after it. Georgia took a few steps after the cat and lay back down in the grass. Sydney was off and running like a bat out of hell, the cat was nowhere to be seen now, but she didn't care; she was free and having a good time. I ran in the house, grabbed her leash and started running after her. Oh, she thought it was play time once again as she scurried between the two fences, through the poison ivy patch and out the back, me chasing her, screaming for her,

her tongue flapping in the breeze, jumping at me then running again. She thought she was just freaking hilarious. Luckily, the people that own the business behind us came out and started to help me call her, and they caught my little minx. Just as I got her on the leash and we are ready to walk back; who should come strolling back there with not a care in the world? GEORGIA. "Hey mom, I heard all the commotion and came to help." "Yeah, she came to help." Georgia managed to unload her collar and leash that I tied her up to out front. I forgot that Georgia was a little escape artist herself, and knew how to get herself loose from her collar. Back through the poison ivy alley we went. Sydney on a leash and me carrying Georgia back to the house.

Another time when I was taking them out for their evening toddle, my father had hooked Sydney up to her leash, but she kept tangling herself up with Georgia. Georgia had to keep stopping to investigate; that was her thing. Sydney just wanted to keep going, so Georgia would sit down as we neared the end of our block. There is an open field that Sydney loves to play in, and there are some woods that I am always fearful that God forbid Syd ever got loose. I would never find her; the underbrush is so thick I could never get through but that little monkey - she could. The tangling war kept up. Then all of a sudden, I realized Sydney was walking a foot ahead of us. I looked down; her leash was off! How she managed that one, the slippery little trickster. She just looked back at me with this little laugh, "Hahahahaha." then she bolted. My God, my biggest fear is that we are right by the woods, but we are also by her field, and she went right for the field. I knelt down trying to hold the end of Georgia's leash under my knee and unfortunately I didn't realize I had knelt down into a plot of poison oak. I called to her; she came running right to me. I grabbed her and she thought I was playing; we were in her field she was rolling around in the grass and the poison oak. I kept rubbing her belly and letting her think we were playing as I snuck that leash back on her collar. Good! I got her under control the little wily one. Just then I heard Georgia barking. I turned around just in time to see Mouth O'l Mighty had gotten loose from underneath my knee and was taking off across the street!

Yes, I hadn't seen her move that fast in years. She was barking her head off because she had seen the dogs in the neighboring yard come out, and she wanted to go say hello. She didn't care that she ran across the street, and I'm sure Old Georgie Girl didn't bother to look both ways either. Sydney and I followed across, the neighbor kids were screaming, but Georgia's bark is so loud that it sounds ferocious although she wouldn't harm a fly - she is just very sociable. I was trying to pull her away from the fence; she wouldn't budge. The neighbors brought their dogs in, but Georgia still wanted to let them know she was out there. I was embarrassed that she wouldn't listen to me when I told her "No," but that is my Georgia. Finally, I got her away from the fence and I tried to get her to walk across the street, but she decided to sit down in the middle of the street. So there we are, all three of us smack dab in the middle of the street; Georgia having a temper tantrum, Sydney howling at her, and me trying to get her to budge - and no one budges the princess when she doesn't want to budge. We must have seemed quite a sight. Georgia finally decided to finish crossing, then she defiantly lay down on a neighbor's lawn and crossed her front paws. By this point I knew she wasn't going anywhere and we were now creating a scene. The older couple that lived in the house next to that one kept coming out and giving me dirty looks and shaking their heads. Like it was any of their business that Georgia was being a brat?

I was so angry now, I didn't know who I was angry at: Georgia for being so incorrigible, Sydney for starting the whole fiasco, the neighbors for their disapproving looks, and not offering a stitch of help and acting so high and mighty, myself for taking them both out at the same time, or my dad for possibly not hooking Syd up correctly. I just sat there pleading with Georgia who just looked at me panting with this look in her eye. "I'm not walking. Not till I'm good and ready". Now I know it's hard for Georgia because she is older, and that she has borderline Cushing's, but I also know a lot of this was a temper tantrum. She had made herself comfortable and Sydney was starting to get very impatient so the only option I had at this point was to carry her and pray that Sydney would be a good girl.

I wrapped Sydney's leash very tightly around my arm so she would be close to me, and would not get loose. Then I leaned down to Georgia and picked the little princess up, swung her around to my side just how I used to hold her when she was a baby, and up the block we went. Past the neighbors who shook their heads in disapproval as we held our heads high and went home. I took Georgia's leash off and put her in the house as I whispered in Sydney's ear, "like a show dog, remember be a show dog" and Sydney and I went right back out of the house and walked right back down the street past the disapproving neighbor's house and Sydney pranced head held high just like a show dog and we both looked over at them and said "Have a Nice Day." Sydney liked putting on the dog so to speak and she could do it well when she wanted and that day she wanted to she wanted to badly. Georgia could do it too; they both had that little show girl attitude in them but out of my three, no one could prance like Sydney.

That was however, the last day I walked them both together, because from now on they would be walked separately and their adventures would have to be contained to the house. They were too much of a handful together.

40

AARON

Although this book is about my girls, and what angels they have been and continue to be, I have to give a special mention to my little step-angel; my little boy that I no longer get to see. My husband and I had separated, and while I was recuperating from my stroke as I had mentioned before, my husband had adopted a rottwieller-shepherd mix that Sydney came to adore. He was the goofiest overgrown lap dog you ever wanted to see. Unfortunately his size, and look, made him rather intimidating, especially to my father - in the beginning.

My ex used to ask us to watch him when he would go on his trips; at the time I was still having seizures from my stroke as they were adjusting my medication. Aaron, like Remi was able to sense this, which made him very special to me. One night as I was laying on the couch in our family room, I was half asleep it had been a stressful day. Our family room had stone floors, and my father was sitting across the room on the loveseat. The girls were scattered about on the floor napping; Georgia closest to my father on her bed in front of the fireplace and Remi sitting next to him watching me on the couch. Sydney and Aaron were resting closest to me on the floor on the other side of the coffee table.

The next thing I remember is Aaron's dead weight on top of me, and my father screaming at him to get off of me. He thought that Aaron was hurting me and Remi lying in between the couch and the coffee table. I was completely disoriented, but at the same time I knew what had happened. I must have dozed off and started to go into a seizure. Aaron sensed it as did Remi and they both kept me safe. Aaron jumped on me (because he was closest) to make sure I wouldn't fall on the floor and crack open my skull either on the coffee table or stone floor, and Remi made sure she got between the coffee table and couch to make sure that if we did start to fall she would block it. Two very smart dogs. Poor Aaron, my father didn't realize it as he was screaming at him to get off of me. Remi knew because if she thought he was hurting me she would have done something about it. My spell passed and I said to my father, "Dad don't you see, he is like Remi - he sensed I was going to have a seizure he saved me. Please don't yell at him." Aaron at this point had gotten off of me and I was petting him lovingly, and Remi too for taking such good care of me. Sydney was over giving her brother/boyfriend a good ear cleaning. I think even Remi and Georgia both gave him a big kiss that night. I know one thing - after that night the girls allowed Aaron to share their mommy's bed - whenever Aaron was a houseguest after that night they made room for him which meant less room for me; but hey, what the heck, he was part of the family now and he should be treated like part of the family. My Ex would say whenever he came home I have to get him out of the bad habits Sydney teaches him. Oh well, I spoil my girls. I can't help it and he got spoiled too when he was with us.

Aaron, the big old loveable galute, we all miss him. Well, Georgia not so much because she is getting to up there in years; but Sydney misses him terribly and

I have many fond memories of him. So does my dad. I miss watching him and Syd play, and I miss the way he would try to climb up on my lap. I just hope that my ex is treating him well, and that he is happy because he is a little Angel. Well for that matter they all are. The last I heard he had a great big yard to run and play in so I'm sure he is happy. Aaron - my little Step Angel.

My Angels, My Girls

41

A RECAP

I'm near the close of my book, a book that really doesn't have a particular ending because life continues for us all. Of course REM REM is no longer with us but there is not a day that I, or my dad, don't think of her. My dad sometimes mistakenly calls Sydney, "Remi" and she will just turn around and give him a look that can turn someone to stone. My Remi, she saved me. She was my protective wolf, the dog that I did not want - the one that I grew to love more than life itself - her death was as if I lost a part of me, lost a child. However, I know her spirit walks with us and she watches out for each of us. She is still the leader of our little pack. We can almost hear her howl whenever there is a full moon, and she would be quite proud of Baby Syd who, after all of her teaching, finally learned to howl properly.

Syd and George miss her too, and they remember her in their own ways. Sydney, whenever you take a collar off of herself or Georgia, she will look to the cabinet where Remi's ashes are kept, and let out a little whimper. She also likes to lay on the loveseat and just stare up at the shelf and look at the pictures, and she loves to talk but only if you start it first. Georgia just stares up at the shelf, and if you bring up REM REM's name she will get this sad little look in her eye and cuddle with you and kiss your hand. Yes, Remi will always be in our hearts and she will wait for each of us to take us to heaven when it is our time so we all can be together again.

Georgia is now 11 years old and, besides her thyroid condition, she is now fighting the signs of old age. After all she is 77 in human years, but she marches on. The queen is still as prissy as ever, but is now on a natural supplement for her arthritis, an antibiotic for a skin infection from her allergies, and an anti-inflammatory for her skin because of her allergies for the summer. My father jokes and says to her all the time. "Georgia, you're on more pills than me!" Georgia just wags her tail and crosses her front paws. Georgia also has to wear booties now because the arthritis has made her legs weak so she has a habit of favoring and developing sores on her back legs, but since we started her on the vitamin supplement it seems to be helping. She has taken over her mother's bed and only allows

My Angels, My Girls

Sydney in it at certain times. She has become quite forceful with Sydney in some ways. It is still hilarious watching those two get on after all these years. She is still the Mouth O'l Mighty watchdog despite her size and ailments, and heaven forbid a cat or squirrel gets into the yard, that little girl is off, arthritis and all. She is definitely, and always will be, a pip.

Sydney is now seven and she is coming into her own, while she tries to copy both REM REM and Georgia. She is the protector of the household she has become undeniably the biggest, most affectionate baby. She has to be around people all the time. She cannot stand to be left alone and she commands attention. Sydney is still trying to get used to her Phenobarbital and unfortunately still has trouble with accidents during the night. I think that is our fault because she doesn't want to wake us up. She is still eating like she has a

330

hollow leg so I have to watch her there, but thank God she hasn't had a seizure, and she doesn't pace as much as she used to. As a matter of fact, she is back to herself; tormenting Georgia much to Georgia's dismay, and playing ball with herself, and playing ball with her Grandpa or me. She won't take no for an answer. She simply throws the ball at us and stares at us until we start playing with her.

She has become a copycat of Remi by sleeping on the loveseat every night and coming up in the morning. I don't know if she does this because of her peeing problem, because she thinks she is protecting the house, or because Georgia has taken over the bed. She also has copied Remi's old counter-surfing habits. Unfortunately for her she was unable to copy REM REM's expertise with this and always ends up getting caught and reprimanded. Baby Syd has also taken over

Georgia's sentry duties as it has gotten harder on Georgia. Sydney now patrols the perimeter of the yard each and every day, but with my little darling I always wonder if she's checking the perimeter or checking for escape routes; after all she is still Syd Vicious the prankster.

One thing that she has started to copy that I do not like at all is a plea for attention. Georgia has skin allergies and she chews on her front paw. I am constantly giving her extra attention - oatmeal baths and the like - giving special attention to her sore, which is now infected, and she has to be on antibiotics. Sydney has been watching all of this special attention that Georgia has been getting, and in turn is a bit jealous - as baby sisters can sometimes be - and now has begun chewing on her paw. Monkey see, Monkey do! "Oh! Look Georgia is getting all this attention because she has a sore. I'll make myself have one too!" Sydney has never had a skin allergy in her life, she just sees and copies. She is an extremely intelligent little girl, but she also wants all the attention and she sees Georgia getting more attention than her sooo… As I said, she has become a baby so now I have two of them chewing on their paws. Georgia chews because she honestly has a problem, but luckily the medication is finally kicking in, but Baby Syd chews on hew paw for attention. Unfortunately, Sydney is getting her paw smacked with a firm, "No!" Every time she starts chewing on it she gives me those sad eyes and a huff. Then she lays down at my feet with her head underneath the end table sucking up all the air conditioning. After pouting she will come up, look at me, tilt her head, I'll pat the couch next to me and she will jump up and start kissing me.

Sydney is my baby. She craves affection. I always call her to come to bed at night but she and Georgia have some kind of understanding now that Georgia gets the bed and that is between them. I'll even howl down to Sydney and she will howl back. We will literally have a conversation in "dog." God knows what I am saying, except that I want her to come up, and she will walk up and across the bed then jump down the other side and go back down. She'll stay up to watch a movie, and for snacks, and come up in the morning and sleep, but the loveseat is her domain from now on.

42

AUGUST 31, 2007

I had to put my poor little girl to sleep last night. She has had some problems recently which we thought were just old age but yesterday she started not being able to breathe well, and her pee was a bright yellow. By the time I got her to the vet there was blood in her urine - an extreme amount. I rushed her to the Emergency Veterinary Hospital where they ran some preliminary tests and put her on fluids and also in an oxygen tent. They came back with a grim diagnosis of Immune Mediated Hemolytic Anemia IMHA (she was destroying her own red blood cells). They told me that this usually is secondary to a tick born or other parasitic infection or cancer but they wouldn't know without a barrage of testing and blood transfusions and immunosuppressant steroids, which would make her prone to other infections. They painted a very bleak outcome, especially for her age. I decided to let my little girl not suffer anymore and I took my last pictures of her as she still tried to be a trooper. Then I held her in my arms, told her it was time for her to go play with Remi and she went to sleep.

I got the discharge papers today. They said that for financial reasons I decided against treatment. I was devastated. They told me she only had a 33 % percent chance of walking out of that hospital. Another 33 % chance that if she did walk out, she would be back within the next 2 months for the same thing. And a 33% chance of being ok. With those odds at her age and with all her other problems; the arthritis, the thyroid, I wasn't putting her through anymore suffering. They have the nerve to write down that it was for financial reasons. HOW DARE THEY! If the vet had told me her condition was any less critical I would have tried. No matter what the cost I would have went into credit card debt. I wouldn't have cared. I told her that. And they have the audacity to put that down. I am mortified.

The discharge papers made it sound like she wasn't that bad off, but that's not the way the vet explained it to me, and not the way she looked struggling to breathe.

I wrote a letter to the Emergency Animal Hospital explaining my feelings about how horrible those discharge papers made me feel. How could they have PUT "Financial Reasons" as the reason for my decision for having to euthanize my poor little Georgie? I was devastated. A couple of weeks went by when I received a letter from the Animal Hospital. The attending veterinarian wrote me a very kind letter explaining that the discharge papers for euthanasia are standard, but because of Georgia's situation she has decided to revamp her way of writing her discharge papers. My little Angel's death was not in vain. There was a purpose. She changed the system of clerical discharge papers regarding euthanasia. Now when euthanasia is involved they take it on a case by case basis so that no other parent will suffer by reading the discharge papers like I did.

It has been almost a year now since I had to put my sweet little Georgia to sleep. It took that long for me to return to the writing of this book. The months following Georgia's death were so trying on all of us:

my father, me, and poor little Syd. Her depression was so intense. People say that animals cannot feel, that animals are just that – animals- but that poor little dog cried for days and would mope around the house, and it took her months before she would get in bed with me because she recognized that side of the bed as Georgia's side of the bed. The side of the bed where Georgia would stare and pray at her candles. Sometimes I swear I still see her shadow over there by her precious statues.

Sydney's depression had everyone worried. We tried spoiling her, taking her to Pet Smart, and even to the designer dog food stores. She would sit with me seat belted in the car, never leaving my side. She was scared to death that someone else would leave her. It got to the point we actually couldn't leave the house without her for a few months. Finally, by Christmas she started to calm down.

43

SYDNEY'S FINAL

HEALTH SCARE

In the beginning of January, I noticed Sydney biting at her paw. My first instinct upon pulling back the fur and seeing this black lump was, "My God she has a tick!" but it wasn't moving. I couldn't get it out so I immediately took her to the vet. Our veterinarian told us, "Oh it just looks like a mole. We can leave it and watch it, and see if it grows, or we can remove it and biopsy it, but it will cost such and such." Now after what we had just been through with Georgia, you better believe I was having it removed. A week later, Sydney was off to surgery and once again she made that long walk down the hall looking back at me like she was never going to see her mommy again...Nothing could compare to when she emerged seven hours later - when I picked her up with the lampshade around her head.

My poor little Syd had three stitches in her front paw and because she loves to lick, she had to have the dreaded e-collar, and she was not happy. My vet thought she was being nice and gave her one with Velcro so that we could take it off of her when she was around us and could be watched. Not a good idea for sneaky Sydney. Sydney figured out that if she banged her head on the furniture enough she could get the Velcro around to the front, and then she could keep pushing her head through until she nosed herself through and then she would be free. She managed to do this about the fourth night into her recovery. I awoke to her with no e-collar and her stitches out. So on a rather balmy January morning, my darling demon child and I took another trip to the animal emergency unit so that we could have her re-stitched. Hahah! They gave her the premier e-collar. No more "out for good behavior" for the next 10 days, and little baby Syd now upgraded herself to antibiotics too. Can you say, "Not happy?" That poor pup walked around for the next three days trying to get that thing off of her head. I kept thinking she was going to end up with a concussion. She finally gave in and settled down.

The results of the biopsy came back. It wasn't a mole at all, but a dark, benign, nevus. Another thing that Huskies are prone to, but my little Angel is fine. I looked into many different health insurances after

Sydney's latest health scare, and I found that some are better than others. One thing I unfortunately did find was that because of Sydney's age - now that she is eight years old an epileptic, with a predisposition to other hereditary conditions - my little girl is basically uninsurable or only insurable at the minimal amount. I was told by one insurance company that I would pay approximately 30 dollars a month and they would insure her up to a $2,000.00 lifetime benefit. And I was told by another that I would pay 20 dollars a month and they would only insure her for poison ingestion and broken bones. I admit I should have insured her as a puppy, but at that time I was given the wrong information, and a lot was going on at the time. Not that I am making any excuses for myself. However, I was told by three other insurance companies she was uninsurable, so my advice to anyone seeking insurance for their pet is get it while they are extremely young, and read the fine print. Especially if your baby is susceptible to any congenital or hereditary conditions, because they may not be covered.

We have an extreme problem in this country when it comes to health insurance. We can't insure two-legged people correctly and it has trickled down to our pets. On the bright side, where our pets, our little babies are concerned, I have found that most veterinarians and animal hospitals will work with you where payments are concerned. Regrettably, they are actually easier to work with than our own health care system, and more humane. The unfortunate aspect of that is some people take advantage, or do so unintentionally and screw it up for everyone else. This is why we should donate to our animal hospitals and shelters because they are there to help us, and the innocents that can't help themselves.

When Sydney was sick I decided to help with her healing by calling in a friend of mine to perform Reiki on her. I figured humans are healed and helped by Reiki all the time and my friend, Reiki Master John King works on humans, but also specializes in helping animals, so I thought, "Why not?" I contacted him through his website, www.DogsLoveReiki.com, he came over and worked on her. Let me tell you, it kept her calm. And I definitely believe that as high-strung as Sydney is, it did help her healing process. Nothing was more comforting than to watch John treat Sydney so gently while she was recuperating from her surgery in January; to hear this giant sigh come from Sydney and know that she was so comfortable and relaxed, and that the Reiki was helping her heal, and helping her deal with that horrible lampshade she had to wear. I swear that the weeks John spent with Sydney left a positive mark on her for life.

My Angels, My Girls

44

SPRING

As we moved into spring, then spring turned into summer, Sydney was back to being her crazy incorrigible self. Sure, there are times when we all miss Georgia and Remi, but you just need to say their names and Sydney looks at you and gives a little whimper. There are times when she goes to the cabinet where their collars and ashes are kept; she will never forget. I will never forget them. They are our Angels in the sky at the Rainbow Bridge, waiting for us and watching over us.

For now, Sydney, my dad, and I go on. We have more adventures; some mundane, some exciting, some tearful, some painful, but one thing's for sure -with Sydney in our lives they will always be unpredictable. Sydney is my spoiled, little, four-legged demon-child with a heart and soul of gold.

45

CONCLUSION

Throughout this book I have voiced a lot of my personal and political opinions on Pet Insurance, Health Insurance, The Courts, Personal Injury Law and Animal Cruelty. These are indeed my opinions and I do not wish to offend anyone in anyway; however, I do wish for people to open up their eyes and not see animals and think, "Oh it's just an animal. It's only a dog. It's only a cat or whatever small - or for that matter - any animal." They are beings with souls and they feel, and they hurt, and they love just like we do. We are all God's creatures. It's About Time We Were Held Accountable for That. We need to stop blaming the animals all the time and delve into the reasons why an incident happened. We need to lobby for stricter animal cruelty laws and tougher penalties; no more slaps on the wrists for people that stage murderous dogfights. Animals have been our lifelines, our companions; they have protected us, helped us, worked with us, and saved us throughout time.

Isn't it about time we stepped up for them?

ABOUT THE AUTHOR

Kellianne Peterson was born and raised in Philadelphia, Pa. She is the only child of Ralph and Catherine Peterson, who passed away on May 6, 1996. Through the years and close friendships she has developed a few pseudo sisters and brothers. Kellianne considers herself an extremely spiritual person with a tremendous love of animals both domesticated and wild alike.

Kellianne currently works as an administrative assistant after many years as a paralegal at a company she feels she can finally call home but writing is her passion. She has had three poems published in different compilations and will continue writing about her little Sydney who has now been deemed "Sydney the Wonderdog" and a woman's fiction book is in the works and possibly her own book of poetry works.

In her down time (which is rare,) Kellianne, enjoys going out to listen to a good band, as music is one of her greatest passions and her first career as she describes (a life time ago). She also enjoys Yoga, daily meditation and avid believer in Reiki and acupuncture.

Kellianne currently resides in Southern New Jersey with her father and Sydney the Wonderdog.

Visit www.MyAngelsMyGirls.com to learn more.

www.ingramcontent.com/pod-product-compliance
Lightning Source LLC
Chambersburg PA
CBHW062359090426
42740CB00010B/1339